MW00622560

REDEFINING

Rich:

8 STEPS TO UNLATCH EMOTIONS FROM MONEY AND CREATE WEALTH

Suzie McLaughlin

SUZIE MCLAUGHLIN

Marie 'Enjoy Suzee'

REDEFINING RICH

Copyright © 2021. Suzie McLaughlin

All rights reserved. No part of this publication may be reproduced, distributed, or transmitted in any form or by any means, including photocopying, recording, or other electronic or mechanical methods, without the prior written permission of the copyright holder, except in the case of brief quotations embodied in critical reviews and certain other noncommercial uses permitted by copyright law.

ISBN: 978-0-578-36365-3

Book Design by Transcendent Publishing

Printed in the United States of America.

Disclaimer: The author makes no guarantees concerning the level of success you may experience by following the advice and strategies contained in this book, and you accept the risk that results will differ for each individual. The testimonials and examples provided in this book show exceptional results, which may not apply to the average reader, and are not intended to represent or guarantee that you will achieve the same or similar results. Names have been changed for privacy protection.

DEDICATION

To Mom and Dad, for always believing in me. I am so grateful
that you have always been there for me – sometimes in tough
love ways, and sometimes in ways that feel like a big, huge loving hug.
I require a little bit of both. I love you both so much and appreciate
your unending support.

CONTENTS

ACKNOWLEDGMENTS

To all my students over my teaching career, YOU are the inspiration for this book! It is my deepest desire that all those who are in the healing arts can live in an abundant state filled and overflowing with love, inspiration, and money. The more we have, the more we can give freely to others from that extra or overflow.

To my family, thank you for supporting me and cheering me on through all the phases of making this workbook come to life. It has been a long journey, and I can't think of anyone I would rather be on it with than you.

To everyone at Transcendent Publishing, thank you so much for helping me during the final, and most challenging, phase of this project. Without you, this book would not have made it out into the world.

Finally, to all of you who read the manuscript during each phase – thank you for your valuable feedback, and for helping me understand what needed to be explained in greater detail. (Not everyone goes to Southwest Institute of Healing Arts!) You know who you are; know too that you are loved and appreciated.

INTRODUCTION

*M*y goal in writing this book was to help people have a clear and straightforward way of dealing with money. It is a topic I know much about; indeed, the following pages largely mirror my own journey to creating a more abundant life. For while I have often been surrounded by people who are quite successful in working with money, I never felt like I understood their secrets.

Financial challenges are common in our society, and they take many forms, depending on one's circumstances. For fifteen years I have been a teacher and a somatic practitioner (or healer), and in both professions it is easy to get a bad taste in the mouth when it comes to the topic of wealth. I experienced this myself, and have observed it in many of my students as they struggled with setting prices for their services. In fact, it often seemed like they were more comfortable being poor or under-charging than they were charging a fair rate that would enable them to create a thriving business and a good life. They would say things like, "What if someone really needs me and can't afford it? I want to be there for those people." This begs the question, is it possible to have a big heart and still be financially abundant? I am here to tell you it most certainly is, and this book contains the tools to help you get there. I know, because I have successfully used them myself to drastically improve my finances, and my life.

For several years I had multiple jobs and tried many ways to build a secure financial future, however, I never really believed I could do it. That, in a nutshell, was the problem, and it often resulted in acts of self-sabotage. I would move forward, building a savings account and even starting to invest, but inevitably a situation or event would occur that sent me sliding backward. What I eventually discovered was that I was carrying, in my mind and my body, many strong negative thoughts and emotions about money that were keeping me from creating a life I could truly enjoy.

This book contains the techniques that will help you reframe how you think about money and build new ways of creating it. Collectively, I think of them as a roadmap to freedom, first by creating awareness of these beliefs, followed by the ability to consciously choose to keep them or create new, more empowering thought processes.

These are not magic bullets, however, but tools that require your commitment and deep, introspective work. Along the way, there will be backtracking and falling out of awareness or flow, but that is all part of the journey. If you keep an open mind and stick with the exercises contained within each chapter, you will be well on your way to creating a life you love and deserve. You will find things like budgeting, paying down credit cards, and other financial tasks will be less intimidating, and reaching for more with confidence is far easier.

That said, this book is *not* about specific strategies for building wealth. There are a plethora of resources out there on this topic, and I have included a list at the end of some helpful YouTubers, bloggers, authors and other financial people who can help you with that part of the journey. Instead, my approach is more foundational and focuses on your money mindset and how it can either be a hindrance or catapult you to success.

Finally, keep in mind that wealth means different things to different people. For some, it is a home to keep their family safe; for others, it is being able to travel and see the world. Still others feel safe and secure only when they have a certain number of dollars in a bank account. There are also different kinds of wealth, such as health and social wealth – or our connectedness to others. Whatever it is for you, the key is to use the sensations in the seven main chakras, or energy centers, in your body to reveal and release your emotional triggers so you can move forward.

Now, are you ready to take your first step towards achieving those financial goals with confidence? If so, then let's get started!

Chapter 1

LEAPING OVER LACK

How Our Thoughts and Feelings about Money Shape Our Financial Reality

How do you think about money? Is it merely a tool to be used to get where you want to go, or is it something more than that? Though it may be hard to admit, for many of us, money is deeply entangled with how we feel about ourselves and even the world around us.

Whenever something connects to our emotions, there is a rather large vibration, or feeling, that surrounds those thoughts. In some cases, that vibration is so pronounced you can actually feel it in your body. It can feel light, like butterflies in your stomach, or heavy, like a tight cord twisting around a part of the body, often the low back.

Low back pain can occur during a time of economic uncertainty, even in people who have never experienced back issues before. Low back issues relate to the first chakra, an energy center in the body that corresponds to a feeling of safety and being grounded in the world. When this chakra is balanced, the person can easily overcome fear. If this energy center is unbalanced, you will feel its vibration in a variety of different ways, from a dull ache to a gripping pain that affects your day-to-day life.

Another example is discomfort in the abdominal region. This often starts in childhood; in fact, it is not uncommon for kids to complain of stomach-aches on the first day of school. Is this a real stomach "bug"? Could be, but more often it is an emotional reaction because they would prefer to stay on vacation! Contrast this feeling of dread to that of a student who is excited about school and feels the tickly, but not unpleasant, sensation of "butterflies." Though very different, both feelings are in the area of the third chakra, the center of personal power. They are a physical manifestation of how someone thinks and feels about the activity to come – in this case, school.

In fact, every sensation you feel in your body presents an opportunity to tune into your thoughts and emotions about a particular situation or aspect of your life, including the flow of money into and out of your hands. If this is a new concept to you, I invite you to open your mind to the possibility so you too can learn what your chakras are telling you. Of course, if you are experiencing pain of any sort, consult with your physician first to see if there is something that needs to be taken care of medically. If you get checked out and the doctor or medical team does not find anything, then perhaps it's time to consider a possible chakra imbalance.

Here is a quick overview of the chakra system, which was first developed in India between 1500 and 500 BC. The word chakra means "center of energy" or "wheel." The seven main energy centers correspond to the nerve plexuses along the spine, though they are believed to reside in the astral plane, just outside the physical body. The nervous system runs on an energetic charge, and I believe that these chakras or wheels of energy interact with that system. This is why working with the sensations of the body is so important, especially when it comes to figuring out what our triggers are.

This system holds many interesting insights that are subtle and powerful at the same time. A great example of this system at work is the sensation of sensing someone is behind you when you can't see them. How can you tell they are there if you can't see them or hear them? This could be your chakra system at work. Even more fascinating is being able to sense how this person is feeling if they, or you, are in a highly emotional state. Now, let's dig a little deeper and explore this way of understanding how the body may be giving us clues to how we could be reacting to money and its use.

The section below discusses the location of each chakra and the issues associated with it. There are also questions to ask yourself about issues you may be experiencing. I suggest keeping a journal to help you process these questions; however, if writing is not your thing, consider dictating your thoughts into your phone using voice memos or some other recording app. In any case, looking deeply into these questions can open whole new ways of understanding, and working, with your relationship to money.

The First Chakra

Located at the "root," or base of the body, the first chakra is where our bottom meets a chair. It is depicted as a wheel or circle, and the color is red. When this chakra is out of balance (in the money realm), it can show up as low back pain or upset in the intestinal part of the digestive system. One explanation of the chakra system is that there are two aspects of each chakra, those being shadow and light. When this chakra is balanced, or in the light aspect, we are in a state of acceptance; when it's out of balance or in the shadow aspect, there is resentment or rigidity.

Let's play with this concept. Here are some questions to ask whenever you feel tightness or pain in this area. Notice if this feeling occurs after a thought or interaction with money.

1. Do I resent any person, place, or thing? Do I perceive that person, place, or thing as the reason I am not where I want to be financially?

_____

_____

_____

_____

_____

_____

_____

_____

_____

2. Is this thought true? If yes, how do I change the situation? If this thought is not true, go to Question 3.

_____

_____

_____

_____

_____

_____

_____

_____

_____

_____

3. What would it take to accept this situation and find a new perspective on "how things are"?

_____

_____

_____

_____

_____

_____

_____

_____

_____

_____

_____

_____

Note: answering this question requires "big picture" thinking.

Here is an example of how Kendra[1*] worked through the above questions.

Kendra has been in the same job for ten years. She has done well and now is at the top of her earning potential at this company, yet she feels under-appreciated and that she is not valued for her contributions. Kendra has been feeling this way for over six months, and those feelings are starting to show up physically as a low back ache that will not go away.
Here is how Kendra might work through the above questions.

1. Do I resent any person, place, or thing? Do I perceive this issue as the reason I am not where I want to be financially?

Kendra's response: I resent the fact that I can't get any more raises even though I feel I am more valuable, given my experience and contributions,

---

[1*] All names have been changed to protect people's privacy.

than colleagues in my position. I feel I deserve to be paid more. The company and my boss do not value me.

2. Is it true?

Kendra's response: Well, no, not entirely true. My boss *does* value me. I feel that. But the company is big and my boss's hands are tied. The company is keeping me from earning more money. **Is that true?**

Yes, this *is* true. The company is keeping me from earning more and getting to where I want to be financially.

3. What would it take to accept this situation and find a new perspective on "how things are"?

Kendra's response: I could choose to stay where I am and feel comfortable, and either change my spending habits so earning this amount is acceptable or investigate other ways to earn money (i.e. get a second job on the weekend or apply for another position that would allow me room for growth). I can also look for another, better-paying job at another company.

Can you relate to Kendra's situation? If so, can you tune into how the sensations in your body shift as you work through it with her?

_____

_____

_____

_____

_____

_____

_____

_____

_____

_____

The Second Chakra

This chakra is located just above the pelvic bone and below the belly button, right over the sexual organs of the body. Its color is usually orange. When this chakra is in balance you will find that you feel "in the flow." Ideas come quickly, as do ways to implement them. We find ourselves being creative in overcoming any hurdles concerning the flow of money and creating what is wanted or needed. This is a fun and relaxed place to be.

When the second chakra feels out of balance (in the money realm), it can result in guilt, feeling of being manipulated or being overly passionate about something that we feel we need or want. When money issues are speaking through this chakra, you may find yourself saying, "I feel like I've been kicked in the gut!" or "I want this so bad I can taste it!"

Questions to consider:

1. What thought, or feeling is creating this discomfort?

_____

_____

_____

_____

_____

_____

_____

_____

_____

_____

2. Is it guilt?

_____

_____

_____

_____

_____

_____

_____

_____

_____

_____

3. Am I feeling manipulated by someone or something?

_____

_____

_____

_____

_____

_____

_____

_____

_____

_____

4. Am I needing or wanting something too desperately?

_____

_____

_____

_____

_____

_____

_____

_____

_____

_____

_____

5. If the answer is yes, would I be able to live without this thing? If so, it is probably a want; if not, it may be an actual need. If it is a need, how soon do I absolutely need it?

_____

_____

_____

_____

_____

_____

_____

_____

_____

_____

_____

Here is an example:

Sam likes to move fast in life, often pushing the edges of whatever he is pursuing. He enjoys feeling the adrenaline rush of going further or faster than many other people would be comfortable with. This way of being has served Sam well and he loves his life ... except when he doesn't. Sometimes, going fast means making moves he feels guilt or regretful about later. One of these moves was buying an adventure vacation before really researching it. As soon as Sam pressed the "buy" button on the website, he felt the twinge in his gut. He decided to research further and found that this company did not live up to its hype and what's worse, many people had been injured because of poor safety protocols for the adventure part of the trip. Fortunately, he was able to receive a refund before it was too late – all because he had listened to that twinge.

Here is how Sam worked through these questions:

1. What thought, or feeling is creating this discomfort?

Sam: As soon as I pressed the buy button, I got that "punch in the gut" feeling. This made me slow down and examine my actions.

2. Is it guilt?

Sam: Nope, I have budgeted some money for an action/adventure. No guilt involved here.

3. Am I feeling manipulated by someone or something?

Sam: Something about the website seemed too good to be true. Because I got the kick in the gut sensation, I decided I needed to research this company more deeply. My gut said something wasn't right.

4. Am I wanting or needing something too desperately?

Sam: Yes, I think I have gone too long without having an adventure vacation and that made me too quick to pull the trigger on this one. I need to make sure I regularly schedule adventure vacations so I don't feel so desperate to find a vacation quickly. Maybe create a list of well-researched vacations I can pull from when the time is right.

Note: second chakra issues tend to come up when money is involved, whether it concerns one's earnings, as in Kendra's case, or a big purchase (i.e., cars, houses, vacations), as in Sam's case. Also, it can physically manifest as a constant ache or that punch in the gut, so be sure to listen to your body and move forward only once you have sorted through all the above questions.

The Third Chakra

The third chakra, located above the belly button and just below the ribs, is all about personal power. Its color is yellow. If you feel like you have a hard time breathing or your ribs feel tight, this chakra may be activated.

If the third chakra is negatively activated, it could be surrounding thoughts of anger or jealousy. For example, you might get this sensation if someone moves forward with an idea that was originally yours, or if you simply want what others have. It may also have to do with greed. Rabbi Benjamin Blech once said, "Greed will always leave you dissatisfied because you'll never be able to get everything you desire. Greed never allows you to think you have enough; it always destroys you by making you strive ever harder for more."

If this sensation occurs when something positive is happening, it could equate to a major or important commitment. People often feel this area tighten when they are stepping out of their comfort zone, perhaps buying a house or moving to a different part of the country or world.

Questions to consider:

1. Is this gnawing sensation in my gut because I am acting outside my comfort zone?

_____

_____

_____

_____

_____

_____

_____

_____

_____

_____

2. If the answer is yes, am I willing to push forward?

_____

_____

_____

_____

_____

_____

_____

_____

_____

3. Is this gnawing sensation in my gut because I feel I do not have enough?

_____

_____

_____

_____

_____

_____

_____

_____

_____

_____

4. Do I feel safe and stable now?

_____

_____

_____

_____

_____

_____

_____

_____

_____

_____

_____

5. What would it take to have a feeling of safety in this financial situation or decision?

_____

_____

_____

_____

_____

_____

_____

_____

_____

_____

_____

Here is the example:

Sally has recently graduated from college and wants to get a fresh start in another part of the country. She put a lot of thought into where she wanted to be and eventually chose the Southwest, as she is tired of winters and wants to experience a place that is warm year-round; she also investigated job possibilities and saw some great prospects in this area of the country. She made the move with five suitcases and enough money for a three-month safety net so she had time to find a job, which helped her feel excited and ready to start her new adventure. Surprisingly, once she got there, she found it hard to breathe! Sally was experiencing a major third chakra activation, or flight from her nervous system, and needed to recenter. Here is how she moved through these questions and found a way forward with her new life.

1. Is this gnawing sensation in my gut because I am acting outside my comfort zone?

Sally: YES! I can't believe I am doing this. Maybe I should just go home. I am suddenly frozen with fear.

2. If the answer is yes, am I willing to push forward?

Sally: I have dreamed about doing this for a long time. If I go back home, then what? No adventure and just more trudging along in life. I can do this. I just need to breathe and follow my plan, one step at a time. Yes, I am willing to push past this feeling and move forward, no matter what it takes.

3. Is this gnawing sensation in my gut because I feel I do not have enough?

Sally: I feel like I have enough, but I have no place to live yet and no car. This is overwhelming to me. I feel ungrounded and without a safe place to land. First thing is to find a car, then a place to live. At least my Dad is here to help me get settled; I will always be grateful to him for coming with me at the start of this adventure.

4. Do I feel safe and stable now?

Sally: Not yet, but I will when I find a car and a place to live. I also need to find a local bank to keep my money. I am not sure what else I will need, but I will find out and create steps to get there.

5. What would it take to have a feeling of safety in this financial situation?

Sally: I feel like I have enough savings to make this work. I have worked out what the beginning expenses would be and still have enough to give myself three months to find a job. Okay, I will be okay. I just need to take this one step at a time. This is going to work. I feel so much better and can breathe easily now. I will create a new life here in the Southwest!

The Fourth Chakra

This chakra, which is green in color and located over the heart, is one of the most well-known and commonly felt. In fact, it can be felt so strongly that some people think they are having a heart attack. (Please note that is also a type of heart condition known as "the broken heart syndrome," caused by acute stress. Most people recover, but it's important to get checked by a physician if you have symptoms.)

You might feel this sensation when you are helping someone out financially or donating money to a charity. What you are feeling is the compassion of the heart. It might feel warm and expansive.

If you feel this sensation in a difficult or negative situation, it may be caused by fear or attachment to an object or person. This feeling can be tight, restrictive, cold or overly hot.

Questions to consider:

1. Is this sensation I am feeling around or in my heart coming from compassion?

_____

_____

_____

_____

_____

_____

_____

_____

_____

_____

_____

2. Is this sensation I am feeling around my heart coming from fear or attachment to a person, place, or situation?

_____

_____

_____

_____

_____

_____

_____

_____

_____

_____

3. If it involves a person, do I need to open a dialogue with the person?

_____

_____

_____

_____

_____

_____

_____

_____

_____

_____

Jon's Story

Jon finds joy in giving money to people in need. He listens to (feels) his heart when deciding who to gift. When his heart feels expansive, he has confidence that his gift will be helpful and move things forward in a positive way for the person receiving it. He has even created an account specifically for this purpose, which he calls his "Joy Account." Sometimes it is given to a particular person for a particular reason; other times it is a more random, "pay it forward" situation. In any case, Jon uses the sensation he feels in his heart region to guide his gifting and to create more joy for himself and others. Though Jon is great at giving, however, he finds it difficult to receive. In the past when he was offered monetary help, it was conditioned upon his using it the way the giver thought was the "right" way. As a result, whenever he is offered help in the form of money, he experiences a contraction in his heart. It stems from the fear that there may be "rules" around accepting the gift. Jon wants to expand his giving, but because of this challenge he has been unable to implement his ideas for his Joy Account. Here is how John worked through the above questions.

1. Is this sensation coming from compassion?

Jon: No, because it feels constricted and small.

2. Is this sensation coming from a place of attachment to a person, place, or situation?

Jon: I feel restricted because the donation is not being given freely. There are rules placed around the giving. I feel as if I am not trusted to use the money in a way that moves things forward toward a positive outcome.

3. If it involves a person, do I need to open a dialogue with them?

Maybe I will tell the giver that I feel I am not trusted and see what they have to say. Yes, it feels good to open that dialogue. I may be surprised by their answer. It is worth a try.

The Fifth Chakra

Known as the throat chakra, the fifth chakra is blue in color and is located right over the Adam's apple or thyroid. The throat chakra can also be felt in the back of the neck. It is common for people to have throat issues (i.e., laryngitis) if there is something they need or want to say and are not saying it. Another common issue for a closed fifth chakra is neck pain.

If this chakra is in balance, a lightness or expansive sensation will occur as you are speaking your truth. Pay attention the next time you ask your clients or your boss for more money, even if it is your true worth for the work you perform.

If the fifth chakra is out of balance it will feel restricted, leading to an abruptness or denial of the truth in any situation you are experiencing. An example could be responding curtly to your boss when he asks you to stay late without extra pay for your time.

Questions to consider:

1. Am I speaking from a place of truth in this money exchange?

_____

_____

_____

_____

_____

_____

_____

_____

_____

_____

2. Do I feel valued, or do I deny myself my true worth?

_____

_____

_____

_____

_____

_____

_____

_____

_____

_____

_____

Tisha's story

Around the same time each year, Tisha experiences laryngitis. Tisha is a thought leader and often speaks in front of large groups of people. She loves this work so much that often she speaks for free, even at events that people pay to attend. She knows she deserves to be paid for her time and expertise but has a hard time speaking her truth when it comes to money.

Because she gets laryngitis every year at the same time, she misses out on opportunities that give her more exposure and greater income opportunities. Tisha is getting really frustrated and wants to get to the bottom of the issue that is causing this block.

1. Am I speaking from a place of truth in this money exchange?

Tisha: No, the truth is, I need to stand up for myself and start asking for a fee for my speaking engagements. My speaking draws crowds and that has value. What I have to say has value for the people receiving it. My speaking for free has become too easy to slide into and it is causing me to become overtired and literally lose my voice.

2. Do I feel valued, or do I deny myself my true worth?

Tisha: Bottom line, I am not valuing myself enough. I need to take a hard look at why I don't ask for a fee, or a higher fee when appropriate. If I start to do that consistently, I will be speaking for people who value what I have to say and I will have more time in between to take care of myself and give my voice the rest it needs. I am ready to commit to doing only two unpaid speaking engagements a year. This way, I will really gauge whether the engagement is worthy of my time or if my time would be used better in another way. For all other engagements I will require a payment that lines up with the value that I am bringing to the event.

The Sixth Chakra

This chakra, which is known as the "third eye" and is indigo in color, resides between your eyebrows and causes a tingling sensation there or at the top of the head. When this chakra is balanced, intuition becomes clear and easy to follow. If out of balance, a headache or tightening around the head or between the eyes can occur.

This imbalance can also show up as confusion, indecisiveness, and maybe even depression. For example, you might find yourself unable to make a decision about something important in your life such as whether to buy a house or take a new job that is offered to you.

Questions to consider:

1. Is my confusion and inability to decide because of a mistaken idea I have about money?

_____

_____

_____

_____

_____

_____

_____

_____

_____

_____

2. Is it based on my belief that I am unable to work well with money?

_____

_____

_____

_____

_____

_____

_____

_____

_____

Henry's Dilemma:

Henry has just been offered a job that will pay him three times more money than he has ever made before. He is excited, but also apprehensive because taking the job means moving across the country – a big change for him and his family. He wonders if this job is too good to be true. What if he takes the job and it is not what he expects? What if he disappoints his new employers and they fire him? Would he be better off staying where he is?

1. Is my confusion and inability to decide because of a mistaken idea I have about money or the value of my contribution?

Henry: Is this company on the "up-and-up"? I find it so hard to believe that any company would pay this amount of money for what I do. Are they going to ask me to do things I don't want to do and expect it because of the amount I am being paid? People with this much money cannot be trusted. Wait… is that true? I did my research and it shows they are an upstanding company, so what is the real issue here?

2. Is it based on my belief that I am unable to work well with money?

Henry: Maybe this apprehension is the overwhelm I am feeling about having this kind of income. This will change a lot for my family for the better, but what will the rest of my friends and other family members think? Am I afraid I will blow this opportunity, or that others will think I am in another realm and come to me with their hand out? What has got me so scared? I think I need help in dealing with this level of income and should start researching professionals, for example, financial advisors and/or abundance coaches, who specialize in this type of work. This way, I'll know someone I trust has my back and I can focus on doing my job well. Yes, I can do this!

The Seventh Chakra

This is the crown chakra, which is white or rainbow-colored, is associated with communication with your higher power. It sits at the top of your head, where a baby's fontanel (soft spot) is located; however, it is harder than others to delineate in the body, so at times you may experience it as "goose bumps" or a whole-body tingle.

If the crown chakra is in balance, you will have a feeling of boundlessness, and the ability to see the big picture. Things that once upset you will not bother you as much or not at all. Unbalanced, this chakra can be the source of grief or deep sadness. Physically, it could be felt as a whole-body ache.

Questions:

1. Am I looking at this experience or decision with the "big picture" in mind?

_____

_____

_____

_____

_____

_____

_____

_____

_____

_____

_____

_____

2. Am I looking at it as having already disappointed me before it ever happens?

_____

_____

_____

_____

_____

_____

_____

_____

_____

_____

_____

_____

Example:

As a young adult, I had lots of time and not much money. This was fine because I was able to make choices that made me happy and create a life that was just right for me. Yet occasionally, I would find myself in a spot where I wanted (shoes, for example) or needed something and didn't have the money for it.

Back in the day, when college graduates automatically received a credit card with a low limit (let's say $500.00), I would use this credit card whenever I found myself a bit short. As time passed, the amount due kept going up. I was paying the minimum but couldn't afford much more than that. Before I knew it, I was hitting my limit.

Now going to the mailbox was like receiving a death sentence because I knew there would be a bill in that box that I didn't know how I would pay. I often felt sick to my stomach and had headaches. These feelings were caused by a thought vibration or sensation of lack. I was questioning my ability to work with money.

Then, one day, I found in that mailbox an answer to a prayer: my grand-mother had sent me a check for $500.00! What happened next is an example of a whole-body shift, starting from the crown chakra and moving down. I fell to my knees, shaking, and began to cry – it was a release of the fear and the feeling of not being enough I had been carrying around.

Oftentimes these major shifts use up a lot of our energy, and this was the case with me – after the emotional release, the feeling in my body was one of relief and exhaustion. I paid attention to the sensations and their locations and realized that what was most important to me was feeling safe and empowered. That insight led me to use the gift money for the credit card bill and not for the new clothes I wanted, which enabled me to get out of debt and back on solid financial ground.

Here is how I worked through the above questions:

1. Am I looking at this experience or decision with the "big picture" in mind?

Me: I was not looking at the big picture when I was using the credit card to get extras or things outside my ability to pay. I did not understand the spot that would put me in financially and emotionally. Going forward, I will pay attention to the big picture and whether a purchase fits into that picture or not.

2. Am I looking at it as having already disappointed me before it ever happens?

Me: In the above case, I was lacking the ability to wait and save for my wants. If I had it to do again, I would look at ways to make additional money for those wants and really look at whether the purchase was worth it. I can't tell you how many times I have had buyer's regret after making an impulse purchase. I continue to work on taking time to decide if what I want is worth the purchase price.

Take a minute and think about money in the form of your income. Imagine receiving a paycheck or opening your online bank account portal to look at your balance. Now, answer the following questions:

1. Look at your bank balance, now close your eyes. Where in your body to you feel sensation(s)?

_____

_____

_____

_____

_____

_____

_____

_____

_____

_____

2. How would you describe the sensations you feel? Is it a feeling of flow and safety or is it tight and uncomfortable?

_____

_____

_____

_____

_____

_____

_____

_____

_____

3. If you did not feel any sensations, you are not alone. Sometimes it takes a bit to feel into the body, or you may just feel more comfortable with thoughts. Is there a thought that pops into your head when you look at your bank balance? If so, start writing down those thoughts to become more aware of them.

_____

_____

_____

_____

_____

_____

_____

_____

_____

_____

_____

I have found that the more framework I have to understand the sensations in my body, the easier it is to decode what my body is trying to tell me. One way to make sense of these feelings is to explore Maslow's Hierarchy of Needs, which was developed by Abraham Maslow in 1943 to assist in explaining human motivation. We will be using it as another tool to try to decode what our body sensations are trying to tell us, specifically when it comes to what may be motivating our spending habits and ways that we work with money. Maslow's Hierarchy of Needs has four basic stages:

1. Physiological and Safety: air to breathe, food, drink, shelter, a safe place to sleep and, finally, freedom from fear.

Many of us go in and out of this stage. Here are some examples of thoughts that can take us there:

- I feel like I am going to be fired with the next mistake I make.
- My job is not secure, and I am always afraid of not having a job.
- There is never enough money to pay all the bills.
- I need to find another job.
- I need to get a raise, but my company is struggling. I am afraid to ask for the money I deserve. If I ask, I may lose my job.
- I can't make my rent. I will get kicked out of my place.
- I can't pay all my bills; I must choose which ones to pay this month.

If these are our thoughts, then we have not yet met our base security needs within our own mind, which triggers feelings of not being safe. You can see how easy it is for our emotions to play with our reality. Start to become aware of your thoughts and pay attention to what happens because of them.

One of my favorite ways to release these thoughts and feelings is to lay cash out on the bed and roll on it, saying, "There is more where this came from!" Silly? Yes! That is the point. We are trying to rewire our beliefs and thoughts. One of the most effective ways to accomplish this is by doing something silly and fun that makes us laugh.

If rolling in money does not appeal to you, you might keep an envelope with cash in your house. Each time you put money in or take it out say, "There is more where this came from." Each time you do this you are creating a new habit, belief and thought process to replace the feeling of not having enough.

2. Love and Belonging: These needs include friendship, relationships, affection, or feeling a part of a group. This can be colleagues, friends, family, or any group in which you feel you are a contributing and accepted member.

Community is essential for our wellbeing; however, it can go either way. If you are in a group and you suddenly get more successful, you may have changed your way of being in that group, and that can make people uncomfortable. If you are not where you want to be financially, the people surrounding you may be contributing to a mindset that keeps you from moving forward. We will talk more about this in Chapter 2.

Thoughts that may be coming from the love and belonging space include:

- I want to try out a new venue, but my friends are resisting that and want to go to the same old hangout. Why won't they try something new?
- The gang went to a party without me. They said they thought I wouldn't want to go because it wasn't elegant enough. Have I changed that much?

If either of these causes an emotional reaction, or if you had judgmental thoughts about them, Chapter 2 will be helpful in working through these challenges around love and belonging.

3. Esteem: These needs include achievement, mastery of a skill, self-respect, and respect for others.

There is nothing more satisfying than mastering a skill. The feeling of accomplishment and self-respect for a job well done is unmatched in the realms of positive emotions and sensations. It can also bring us to a whole new level of earning potential. On the other hand, if we fail it can stop us in our tracks.

Releasing our fear of failure is something we need to practice repeatedly, and we do this by trying something new and pushing past our boundaries. It is not that the fear necessarily goes away, but it stops controlling us and instead becomes a marker of something big. Instead of giving up, we know how to go full steam ahead, if it will help us reach our goal.

Here are some examples:

Dave, a musician, wants to send an audition file to a popular venue, one that has a bigger stage and pays more money than he has received for past gigs. But whenever he thinks about it he gets a tight feeling in his chest and throat that is uncomfortable, which stems from his fear that he will be laughed at or ignored. Does he send the audio file anyway? The answer depends on how comfortable Dave is with risk, perceived or real. This is a mental muscle that must be challenged to grow. Dave looks at the downside and the upside of this decision. The only downside is the potential hit to his ego if he is turned down. The upside is that if he is willing to risk disappointment, he will be learning the very valuable skill of being comfortable with temporary discomfort.

Sara is thinking about investing some money. Her family and her friends have never invested, so she is on her own and must take a chance. She does deep research, takes some classes, and learns what she needs to for confidence in her decisions moving forward. She is literally sweating as she goes to talk to a financial advisor. Is this a good sign or a bad one? Sara decides it is a good sign that she is taking a leap of faith to grow her financial base.

4. The Need for Self-Actualization: realizing personal potential, self-fulfillment, and personal growth experiences.

All the other levels of the hierarchy must be met in order to experience this one. If we are able to achieve those levels, even for a short amount of time, we are able to reach for more and experience new levels of self that we may not have dreamed possible.

Here's another example from my own life journey:

I was once asked by my father, "If you had all the money you could ever need and you did not have to worry about making an income anymore, what would you do?" My answer: I would be a perpetual student, soaking in all sorts of ideas and theories from all around the world while traveling to experience different cultures. This is still a big-picture goal of mine.

Time to pull all these ideas together using my experience with debt as a new college graduate from earlier in this chapter. Which of Maslow's stages were addressed? What chakras were activated?

- Stage One (Physiological and Safety Needs): Unable to meet my financial obligations and pay my bills, I felt squeezed, almost literally. Chakras one, three and four were affected. My physical sensations were a backache, heavy heart and tight chest, making it hard to take a full breath at times.

- Stage Two (Love and Belonging): Because I did not feel abundant, I did not go out much and did not have many friends. I began to feel sad and lonely. Chakras two and four were affected. My physical sensations were a heavy heart and tears.

- Stage Three (Esteem Needs): At this point in my life, I did not feel like I had mastered anything! Everything was new and I was making plenty of mistakes. My lack of self-confidence began to paralyze me. The chakras affected were three and five. Physical sensations were stomachache and sometimes headache.

- Stage 4 (Self Actualization): As a college student, I had no idea what self-actualization was. I did not even have this concept in my thoughts for I was just trying to survive. The chakras affected were two, four, five, six and seven. My physical sensations were a heavy heart and back pain.

Your turn! Think of a current or past story that has to do with how you deal with money or when you tried something out of your comfort zone. Write the story down.

_____

_____

_____

_____

_____

_____

_____

_____

_____

_____

Answer these questions:

- At what stage (think Maslow's hierarchy) in this story did you spend most of your time?

_____

_____

_____

_____

_____

_____

_____

_____

_____

_____

- What chakras were affected and where did you experience physical sensations?

_____

_____

_____

_____

_____

_____

_____

_____

_____

_____

- What role does money play in how you experience each of these stages?

_____

_____

_____

_____

_____

_____

_____

_____

_____

_____

_____

This is a great start, but there is so much more to learn. If you must work to keep your nose above water financially, no matter how much you make, you are not rich. On the other hand, if you have no debt and are living within your means; no matter how much, or little, you make, you are living a rich life. Why? Because you have come to a place of empowerment. Once you have found this place, the choices you make will no longer come from uncontrolled fear or lack.

Are you currently living a rich life? If not, know that it is within reach, and that it has less to do with your bank balance and more to do with how you feel about money and being able to pinpoint where you need to change your thoughts and feelings about how it flows through your life. Next up, how to reset your thoughts about money.

Chapter 2

WHAT IS MONEY?

Practical Tips for Resetting Your Thoughts

In the first chapter we explored the different ways our bodies alert us to our thoughts and feelings about money and motivate our financial decisions. Now we are going to get into how we can begin to shift those thoughts and make real changes in our lives. The first step is to understand that money is simply an idea. If you look, you will find evidence of this all around us. Many people are playing with ways to live without money or creating sorts of currencies. Have you heard of bitcoin? This is a digital currency that was developed as an alternative to our current monetary system - basically, it cuts out the "middleman" – i.e. the bank – and is exchanged directly between users. Or how about the restaurants that do not set prices, but ask their patrons to pay what they can? Some people would like to eliminate currency altogether and adopt a bartering system; for example, that same restaurant may trade food for another product or in exchange for a service provided by the patron. While these innovators come from different walks of life, they all share the understanding that money is simply an idea. Now, let's explore this further using the following example.

Since safety and money are often linked, start by answering this question: How much money would it take to make you feel safe? How about a million dollars? Would that amount keep you from fear? Let's look at what a million dollars really is.

I have heard and read many stories of people who received a windfall of a million dollars, only to be left with nothing or, worse yet, be in debt within a few short years. In some cases, it only took the poor souls months to burn through it all. Yes, a million dollars seems like A LOT of money, but the truth is it can slip through our fingers just as easily as spending a hundred dollars on a fun night out.

To get my mind around this, I looked up how much you could earn by having one million dollars in a savings account and accruing interest.

At four percent interest compounded monthly, you would earn the following:

> One day- $109.59
> One month- $3,333.33
> One year- $40,741.54
> Five years- $220,996.59
> Ten years- $490,832.68
> Twenty years- $1,222,582.09

Now, I don't know about you, but I would have thought a million dollars would earn way more than that! Keep in mind that this means the principle (meaning the money that the interest is generated from), must remain at one million dollars.

Could my family and I live comfortably with a monthly income of $3,333.33? I thought about it and, honestly, at this point in my life it would be a tight squeeze. Suddenly, a million dollars just does not seem like so much. It is interesting what perspective can do when looking at money, and from my perspective, a person living off four percent interest is not living an extravagant life.

However, if this person does not have any debt, the situation changes. For example, if I did not have credit card balances and our house and vehicles were paid off, then living off the interest of a million dollars would be possible. But that is quite a few steps into the future for me. How about for you?

Here's the thing: no matter how much money we make it won't be enough if we don't feel that *we are enough*. That feeling of not being enough or that we are lacking in some way is what is really causing us pain. And, as we saw in the case of Kendra and in my own story, it might be a very real physical pain.

In fact, many people who are making six- or even seven-figure incomes feel exactly the way I felt before the miracle check from my grandma arrived – a combination of desperation, fear and dread. Why? Because their feeling of "not-enoughness" drove them to spend more than they make, putting them in debt.

If this is true, how do we make this idea of money work for us? I have found the following suggestions to be especially helpful.

1. Whenever you make a transaction, be sure to think (or, if you're brave, say aloud), "There is more where that came from!"

As I mentioned earlier, I have made this a habit, and find it especially helpful when I am starting to feel that dread or overwhelm – that feeling of "not enough." Some may think the feeling of not enough has to do with not having enough – be it money, time, space, and so on – but it is deeper than that. Again, your bodily sensations can be helpful if you pay attention. The next time the thought "not enough" crosses your mind, take a minute to do a body scan. Do you have a tight feeling in your gut, or maybe you notice your breathing has become shallow? These are clues and opportunities to change your thought pattern. Once you have the awareness of "not enough," you say or think, "There is more where that came from". This resets the subconscious mind to think of possibility instead of fear of lack. It will also calm your nervous system, allowing your thinking mind to react in a logical and calm way instead of panic or low-grade fear, which can lead to very different, healthier choices about money. This simple phrase really works if you use it consistently, just give it a try.

2. If you can, get a big stack of bills, lay them out on your bed, and roll in them, laughing and saying, "I love having all this money!"

This activity may seem silly, and that is exactly why we are doing it. When we do something out of the ordinary, it can reset how we think and feel about a topic – in this case, finances. For me, rolling in cash was a turn-around moment, when I allowed myself to be joyful and grateful for receiving all this money. I even made my husband do it (though he was rolling his eyes). This celebration of literal abundance, and our laughter, helped us create new neural pathways that connect cash flow with joy instead of dread.

3. Be aware of where your money is. Do you carefully keep it, or do you throw it in your pocket or the bottom of your bag? Do you leave money on the floor when you drop it?

The phrase "out of sight, out of mind" pops up when I think about this habit. So often we drift into the feeling that we don't have enough, and forget about all we *do* have. If you went on a treasure hunt, right now, I bet you would find many treasures. Try it. Look in the cushions of your couch, in your car, in your pockets of coats, in your bag and the bags you have stored. You may be surprised how much money you find, how many gift cards you have hiding in your wallet or your desk. All of this is currency; it has been here the whole time, just waiting to be of service. We simply need to bring it into focus, and a treasure hunt is an excellent way to do this. If you have kids, this is an awesome activity to do with them.

4. Treat your money as you would a dear friend.

What do I mean by this? I mean take care of your money. Fold cash nicely and have it arranged in your wallet or your virtual account in an honoring way. Create accounts for different needs or wants such as trips, holidays, clothes, and so on; look at them at least once a week and add to them as you can. If you are taking care of it, that means it has value and those things that have value will multiply. Try it and see what happens.

5. Each day, look at your bank account and, regardless of the amount, speak words of gratitude over it.

We often underestimate the power of gratitude, which is a key ingredient in attracting what we want, including money. As we become present with what we already have and give thanks for it, more will come to us. This is because we have brought our desires to our conscious mind and are therefore more aware of opportunities to bring them into our lives. You can't see the opportunities if you are not looking or are closed off to them. Gratitude helps us get there.

6. Be sure to use any gift cards you have. Money runs in a cycle; it likes to flow in a positive way. If you can't use the cards, give them to someone who can, with a smile and the excitement of being able to give.

This is so important! Be on the lookout for people who could use the cards you know you will not use, and give them freely and with grace. This will not only bring you a joyful feeling, it will also immediately shift you into a feeling of abundance. You are abundant, you have enough to give to others. What a fantastic feeling! Give it a try.

7. If you have any checks you have not cashed, do it today! Keep that money moving in a positive way, into your bank account!

This is another positive habit that brings abundance into your awareness. It is also being a good steward of money that has been given to you. Cashing the check also helps the giver; it lets them know you appreciate and value the exchange and helps them keep their account in order.

8. Any clothes or things in your house you don't use? Give them to someone who can.

This one is interesting for me. Every time I do a major closet clearing, within a month, someone brings me more clothes – and I do mean *every time*. What's more, they are often designer clothes! I feel these experiences are providing me with physical evidence that I am supported, and help me trust that as I move things along to someone else, more will be given to me.

Are you having fun? Good! Positive vibrations attract positive vibrations.

Last step:

Be aware of your language when it comes to money.

Do you ever hear yourself saying, "I can't afford that," or "I don't have enough money to do that?" These words lower your vibration to meet your beliefs about what you are worthy of having.

Think about what you say. Is it true? Is it possible that you *could* afford it, but are choosing not to do or have whatever it is because you want or need something else more? If this is the case, just becoming aware that you have a choice can cause a major shift in perspective. Can you feel the difference in your body?

Try this out:

Close your eyes and think of something you want and say the following:

"I can't afford _____."
Be aware of how it feels, the sensations in your body, when you say that sentence. What is the feeling and where do you feel it?

_____

_____

_____

_____

_____

_____

_____

_____

_____

_____

Now, think of the same thing, but this time say, "I choose to not buy ____
_____at
this time because _____
_____ is more important to me." How does it feel in your body
when you say this?

Can you feel the difference in sensation between the two phrases? This difference is key in changing the way money flows in your life. Money is like the current in a river. Or perhaps it is more like the water cycle. Money can change from fluid in a stream (think cash) to clouds (getting nearer to that paycheck) to beautiful rain (paycheck is deposited into your checking account). Money is always flowing and moving in many ways and forms – from cash to IRAs to bitcoin, real estate and more!

Be aware of how you speak about your spending. Be loving to the currency that comes into your life and remember to have gratitude for all the blessings that have been received.

It's important to keep in mind that the vibration or sensation also works in the other direction. When someone is having a lot of success and gaining a lot of currency, it can become uncomfortable for them. Have you ever witnessed someone becoming successful and then suddenly doing something to sabotage their achievement? Acts of sabotage are an indication that they are uncomfortable with this new vibration and flow of money. Sometimes it happens when relationships with others change as a result of your newfound abundance.

Oftentimes, however, the discomfort lies within you; it is a revisiting of that "not enoughness" feeling. This is known as "imposter syndrome," and it is quite common, especially among successful, highly-regarded people. When you are experiencing a new level of monetary success it can feel unreal. If this is you, give yourself time to settle into this new relationship with money and you will eventually get comfortable with its flow. You may also want to take a deeper look at why you are experiencing imposter syndrome (i.e. a feeling of unworthiness) and work on clearing it.

Take the time to review this chapter as often as needed. Remember, as we travel this life, new challenges will come up. Welcome them and be sure to check in with yourself often. Do you feel empowered or not enough? If it is the latter, use the tools we have covered (or create your own) to reset. Bring yourself back into awareness about your purchases or other financial choices. Are you making them from an abundance mindset, or one of lack?

If you are in a place of empowerment, do you find yourself having to deal with changes and misunderstandings with those closest to you? If so, the next chapter is for you.

Chapter 3

MONEY AND CULTURE

Success and Group Shaming

Life is going well. You have worked hard at changing your empowerment status and have started to turn things around in a big way. So big in fact, that people are starting to notice. People you care about, and who you assume will be happy for you. You may have even discussed finances with them, each sharing your goals of getting to a place of true freedom and financial independence. They always have said they want the best for you, but now you cannot help but feel that something odd is going on. Perhaps you are starting to feel like an outcast amongst the people you love so much. They may start calling you things like "moneybags" when you buy yourself something nice or even tell you that you're getting "too big for your britches," or think you're "all that and a bag of chips." Perhaps they even start "forgetting" to tell you about dinners or other get-togethers. What is happening here?

This behavior is called "group shaming," and it can happen with any group that depends on each other, especially in an emotional or spiritual way. Here's why: when we start to change our vibration around any "idea" (money, in this case), the group can sense it. At first, it causes excitement. Something is new, different, and exciting. However, over time the difference between your vibration and your group's vibration becomes uncomfortable.

This discomfort is the very reason why people can fail financially and "fall back" to where they were before. To feel unsupported and undervalued is so painful that those experiencing it would rather go back to the financial space they were in before than move forward without the group. Of course, this is an unconscious reaction. It will seem as if we are just having a run of bad luck or can never get ahead. Sound familiar?

According to Scripps Howard World News service, over seventy percent of lottery winners lose all their winnings within seven years! How could that happen? Could this be because winners are so uncomfortable in this new life situation that they give away or spend it all? I think it is a strong possibility, and that most of the time they don't even understand what is happening.

The first step to overcoming group shaming is to understand what it is, and that it is *not* a personal attack. On a conscious level, your friends and extended family *do* want you to succeed. As mentioned, the issue here is a difference in vibration, or way of being. It is that new perspective you gain as you start becoming more comfortable with money and its flow to you – which may now be different from that of your friends and family.

If this is the case, you are a trailblazer; you are breaking new ground. The thing is, a trailblazer often must move on their own for a while until the others see the trail, or you bump into a new group who shares your perspective. The key to your continued success is a willingness to "let go" of the need to be validated by your current group. Of course, for many of us this is no small challenge. Why? Because we find comfort and safety in our group, so the thought of moving away from them, even temporarily, can be upsetting and scary. However, we must move past these feelings if we want to change our financial picture and achieve other goals that are important to us.

Try these journal prompts to get this thought process started.

1. Write down all the people who you would consider a part of your group. These people could be family, friends, coworkers, or anyone you spend time with or feel influenced by.

_____

_____

_____

_____

_____

_____

_____

_____

_____

_____

2. Are there any people on the list that you would consider a role model (i.e. a parent) or mentor when it comes to handling money?

_____

_____

_____

_____

_____

_____

_____

_____

_____

3. Is the way they work with money something you want to emulate? (If yes, write down the name(s) and go to Question 4, if no, explore what about them makes you resist wanting to emulate them.)

_____

_____

_____

_____

_____

_____

_____

_____

_____

4. Would they be willing to mentor you in changing your own relationship with money?

_____

_____

_____

_____

_____

_____

_____

_____

_____

_____

5. Which people in your group are always asking you for money, or a
little help?

_____

_____

_____

_____

_____

_____

_____

_____

_____

_____

6. What is their story?

_____

_____

_____

_____

_____

_____

_____

_____

_____

_____

7. What is the "hook" in their story? In other words, what makes you feel like you must help or give money to them?

_____

_____

_____

_____

_____

_____

_____

_____

8. If you help them, do they move forward in an empowered way, or continue to ask for more?

_____

_____

_____

_____

_____

_____

_____

_____

As you review your answers, you will probably see that the group falls into two camps: those who give and those who receive. This is where it becomes challenging. Can you feel your emotions rising to the surface?

This is expected, as the group's power is connected directly to our emotions and our feelings of self-worth. They are reflections, or mirrors into the self. Which question brings up the most emotions? Is it thinking about how your parent never seemed to have enough, or writing about the people in your group who always seem to need something?

In my case, I struggled with asking for help from a mentor. I wanted to do it myself, even though I had yet to be truly successful with handling money. My pride and my fear of seeming weak or stupid got in the way. I also knew I had to be careful about who I chose – specifically, they needed to understand my biggest challenge, which was letting my emotions get in the way when I dealt with money. Sure enough, when I asked the people in my group who were financially successful to mentor me, they responded with confusion. For them, money and emotions were two separate things. It took some time, and really tuning in, to find a mentor who could work with me and help me see what I needed to work on regarding my finances.

Of course, you may not have a potential mentor within your group. What then? This brings us back to the possibility that we may have to move forward without them, at least temporarily. How do we feel when we think about not being with our group anymore? Is there panic, anxiety, big-time fear? If so, it should come as no surprise. We think of our group as our lifeline; it is part of the survival instinct found deep in our genes.

To overcome the power our group has on us and move forward, we need to rewrite the story of our relationship to that group, thus rewiring our thoughts about it. Breaking these emotional ties does not mean we do not love our group anymore. It simply means we understand their fear and know that the direction we are headed is a necessary detour from a trail that is not working for us. The trail our group is on may feel safer, but will not move us toward the life we want to live.

According to Dr. Mario Martinez, a clinical neuropsychologist and author of *The MindBody Code: How to Change the Beliefs that Limit Your Health, Longevity, and Success,* many of us are operating from flawed stories that stem from at least one of three archetypal wounds we experienced in our youth. These wounds include:

1. *Shame*

   Shame is a painful feeling of humiliation or distress caused by the consciousness of wrong or foolish behavior. This behavior is often pointed out by an elder in our group. This wound can make us feel small and afraid to go against authority. At its worst, we take on shame as if it is a part of us. "I am ashamed of _____" is a phrase used by a person who has taken on shame as a part of their personality. On the other hand, the statement "I *feel* shame for the way I treated you" is indicative of a person who is strong in who she is and is owning up to a specific behavior that she would like to apologize for and change in the future.

2. Abandonment

   Abandonment is the action or fact of abandoning or being abandoned. This is a common wound and can make it difficult to trust others, even those close to us. There is often a fear of loss, real or imagined, that can cause negative behaviors such as overreacting to others or circumstances, or engaging in harmful self-talk.

3. *Betrayal*

   Betrayal is the breaking or violation of a presumptive contract, trust, or confidence that produces moral and psychological conflict within a relationship amongst individuals, between organizations or between individuals and organizations. For our purposes here, we are talking about the breakdown of trust between two people.

These wounds were inflicted, many times unintentionally, by authority figures such as our mothers, fathers, teachers, or anyone that we depended upon for survival and/or guidance. Because we love these figures, our wounds get mixed up with love, which creates conflict and fear that we feel deep in our bones when we attempt to blaze a new trail. Moreover, our group will use these archetypal wounds to keep us where we are – again, often without awareness of what they are doing.

Archetypal wounds are also inflicted by our cultures. To find evidence of this, you need look no further than famous trailblazers in history and how they were treated by their communities. Take, for example, Marie Curie, Emelia Earhart, and Rosa Parks – women with very different backgrounds who had one thing in common: they experienced push-back and ostracization from society because they stepped outside the norm. In Rosa Parks' case, her actions were risky and could have even resulted in bodily harm from those who wanted to maintain the status quo. What made her, and the others, persevere? It was a force within that could not be denied, and it propelled them forward despite challenging and sometimes life-threatening times. How each woman accomplished her goal was unique to her, but each person knew that this force was bigger than the self.

Now, here are some questions for you.

1. What is motivating you to blaze a new trail?

_____

_____

_____

_____

_____

_____

_____

_____

2. Are you acting out of love, or fear?

_____

_____

_____

_____

_____

_____

_____

_____

If it is fear, you will know because it will feel heavy and hard. For many people, this feeling will sit in their gut or on the upper back. If it is love, the feeling is uplifting, perhaps a tingling through the body or a feeling of strength or force that makes you want to throw your shoulders back and lean into the next step.

Here is a story of trailblazing to achieve greater income. It was born of fear but became something more.

Sandra had always wanted to be in a place of power, but she was raised in a culture that considered meek and mild girls as "good" and outspoken girls as "troublemakers." Because of this, she was told from an early age that she was a showoff, that she often acted "better than."

Sandra railed against how others perceived her. She knew deep inside that she was meant for big things, yet at the same time she felt shame whenever she spoke her dreams out loud. As Sandra grew, her academic talent became apparent. She was the first in her family and her community to go to college on a full scholarship. Even so, she had to endure the taunts of others. "Make sure you don't get too big for your britches now," they said, or "Just remember where you came from."

Sandra wanted so badly to stand in her own power. She had earned that right by working hard all her life. Behind that work was the driving force that whispered to her all the big things she had to do. That whisper kept her going whenever the doubt of her community crept into her thoughts. Fortunately, Sandra graduated from college with honors and landed a job with a prestigious company. This job came with more money than Sandra had ever thought possible.

Here is where it gets interesting. As Sandra built her new life, she continued to hear the voices of those in her group and in her community. "Remember, don't get too big for your britches," they would whisper, "What, you think you are better than us?" Each time she heard these voices, she would doubt herself and look outside of herself for validation. These validations came in the form of expensive clothes, cars and all the trappings of what Sandra thought she "should" be.

Because Sandra had no real experience working with the amount of money she was earning, she had no idea she had to budget it and soon found herself in serious debt. With each poor decision the fear mounted until it was a major player in her life. "See," the fear would say in her mind, "You got too big for your britches and now you are in deep trouble. You need to go back to being small, where it is safe."

Fear kept Sandra from talking to any of her new friends. Shame kept her locked tight in her mind, where the old thoughts could take over. Fear kept her spending beyond her means, so she could appear to be doing well and "be happy." Can you relate to this story? If you can feel this fear in your gut, you may have something in common with Sandra.

Just for fun, let's look at this same story, but change the perspective. Instead of focusing on fear, what might happen, if Sandra's thoughts came from a place of love?

Sandra was outspoken as a girl and had lots of big ideas, but these ideas would often be shot down by the people in her community. Even so, Sandra was lucky, because she had people in her life who believed in her.

They encouraged her ideas and helped her voice them in a positive way that could easily be heard by others. Sandra learned to come from a place of love and deep compassion. It was modeled for her by those she admired. Because she had this support and scaffolding to work from, she was finally able to deflect any attempts from her larger group or culture to shame, abandon, or betray her.

Sandra grew into a strong, self-confident, risk-taking young woman who did not easily give up on the ideas that came to her. She was resilient and able to keep going when a project or the people in her life put up blocks. In fact, she came to see these blocks as opportunities for reflection. She would look at what she was doing and assess if the opportunity was worth pursuing further, or if it was time to switch direction.

Sandra was grounded in love and self-empowerment. These two components allowed her to venture into unknown territory with anticipation and excitement instead of fear and dread. Coming from a place of love and self-empowerment always stands an individual on solid ground. It is so much easier to take a risk if you know that the risk is only temporary, and that love and empowerment are truly always at the core.

Babe Ruth, a baseball player for the Boston Red Sox, understood that. He knew what he wanted, and he didn't care what other people thought. His motto was, "Never let the fear of striking out get in your way." To this day, Babe Ruth holds the record for strikeouts at-bat. He also holds the record for the most home runs (forty-plus!) per season of playing – all because he did not let fear get in his way.

Are you ready to be like Babe Ruth or the self-empowered, love-based version of Sandra? Would you like to resist being influenced by your culture or your group when you know in your gut that the group's way of thinking is not helping you blaze a new trail?

Here is a tool to assist you in getting to a place of love and self-empowerment. You may find yourself returning to this tool time and again. For many of us, this is onion work, meaning we need to peel layers away to get to the core of our fear-based thinking.

Remember, be kind to yourself and take this one step at a time, at your own pace.

Step 1:
First, let's delve a little deeper into the archetypal wounds of shame, abandonment, and betrayal.

Shame brings about internal feelings of inadequacy, dishonor, and regret. The main characteristic of this emotion is internalized feelings, such as *"I am bad"* as opposed to *"I feel bad."* The "I am" statement sig-nifies that one is identifying the self as the feeling, which makes it much more difficult to move out of and can lead to behaviors to help them "get away" from the feeling. These include addiction, withdrawal from others, or behaviors that attempt to mask the behavior that is seen as shameful.

Abandonment represents a core human fear. It is a cumulative wound containing all the losses and disconnections we've experienced, dating back to childhood.

Abandonment can be:

- A feeling of isolation within a relationship.
- An intense feeling of devastation when a relationship ends.
- Aloneness, not by choice.
- Someone over the age of 60 being "Put out to pasture" by the company as if obsolete.
- A person feeling without purpose due to the loss of a job and/or the children moving out of the family home and into their own lives.

Abandonment's wound is at the heart of a variety of human experiences and unique to each person. It can also manifest as rage that we turn against ourselves. We abandon ourselves, which can slowly drain our self-esteem, causing sadness, self-doubt, insecurity, self-sabotage, and fear – sometimes indefinitely.

Betrayal is the sense of being harmed by the intentional actions or omissions of a trusted person. The most common forms of betrayal are harmful disclosures of confidential information, disloyalty, infidelity, and dishonesty. The effects of betrayal include shock, loss and grief, morbid preoccupation with the betrayer, damaged self-esteem, self-doubt and anger, both toward them and ourselves for trusting them.

Notice that each of these core wounds will cause the individual experiencing them to turn harmful thoughts and feelings against the self. This is what makes them so powerful and can cause a person to fall short of what they are capable of in their life.

What wounds do you suspect you might be carrying around?

_____

_____

_____

_____

_____

_____

_____

_____

_____

_____

_____

_____

_____

Step 2:

Start a journal or log of any memories you have of being shamed, abandoned, or betrayed. Every time a memory surfaces, record it in your journal.

Let's try it right now. Think of one memory that comes up for you regularly and creates a feeling of shame, betrayal, or abandonment. If you are not sure how to do this, think of a story you recall when someone asks about your childhood or about someone you looked up to as a child.

_____

_____

_____

_____

_____

_____

_____

_____

_____

_____

_____

_____

_____

_____

_____

_____

Step 3:

Look at this memory and determine the appropriate archetypal category.

1. Does the memory create a feeling of shame, abandonment, or betrayal?

_____

_____

_____

_____

_____

_____

_____

_____

2. There may be more than one category showing up in a memory. Simply put an "S" for shame, an "A" for abandonment or "B" for betrayal beside each part of the story that raises emotions for you. Emotions or bodily sensations can point us toward what is truly shifting our reality.

Now, count the letters. Which category has the most memories?

You'll focus on the most active category in Step 3.

Step 3:

When you are ready, read one of the memories from the most active category. Pay attention to where you feel the memory in your body, as this will serve as clues as to how this memory may be influencing you today.

For example, if you have these same physical sensations when making a financial decision, chances are a memory is influencing your choice. Give yourself time to make this awareness a habit. Seek to become aware of when memories are influencing your decisions.

1.What is the body sensation that comes with an active core memory?

_____

_____

_____

_____

_____

_____

_____

_____

_____

Step 4:

Once this awareness becomes a habit, you can change your perspective.

Here is an example of this process in action:

Jana was actively working on changing her response to feeling ashamed, which stemmed from several events that happened when she was a young girl. She realized that she could actually feel this emotion, like a heavy weight or blanket, on her upper back, which was very helpful when she was making a decision.

When she felt the sensation of a heavy blanket or cape on her shoulders, she trained herself to stop what she was doing. Jana would either write down what was happening when she had this sensation or, if there was a flash of memory, write down the memory. She would then take the time to work through the memory from her current reality, looking at the memory as if she was watching a movie. This helped to reduce the automatic emotions involved in this stored memory.

As she did this, over and over, the process became faster, and it was easier to identify when "the cape" was coming into play. Jana was starting to feel empowered. She now understood that her past did not have to influence the present moment. She was free to make a new choice.

Each time Jana caught herself experiencing this old feeling of shame and instead chose from a place of self-love and empowerment, a whole new world opened to her. She was able to take more significant risks and was no longer paralyzed by the unknown, or how others might perceive her. Of course, this took time and a lot of practice, but eventually she became more adept at sensing what was occurring in her inner world. That hard, heavy cape transformed into a superpower, reminding her that another, more desirable path was available to her. Now, whenever she experienced the cape sensation, she would say to herself, "I choose what will empower me" and continue moving toward the life of her dreams.

One day, Jana went shopping for a new outfit. She had recently lost some weight and wanted to celebrate with clothes that fit her new body. As she tried on clothes that were a smaller size, she noticed that feeling of the cape and stopped to explore what was happening beneath the surface. She discovered that buying clothes that fit her body was bringing up shame-filled thoughts from long ago. In high school she liked to wear clothes that fit well and that brought attention from guys and shaming from girls – a double-edged sword that had caused a very deep wound.

If Jana hadn't done this work, she may have felt "the cape" while shopping and unconsciously associated it with the price of the clothes. This could have sent her into a spiral of there is never enough, other people have more, and so on. She may have not bought any clothes and gone home placing her anger on the cost of the clothes. This is a form of projection that can happen when we are unconsciously trying to protect ourselves from painful experiences that happened in our past and remain stored deep in our memory.

Instead, because she has trained herself to work with the sensation of the cape, she was able to recognize the trigger and consciously choose to clear out the baggage of the past – first by lovingly acknowledging the memory from a higher perspective, then understanding that those who had shamed her were young people trying to define themselves, and, finally, forgiving them. This made it easier to release the shame associated with this memory, step into her power as her present self, and enjoy picking out an outfit that showed her personality, joy, and the healthy body she now inhabited.

This work is challenging and does take time, but it is so worth it once the new tools and habits have been set and become a new awareness to work with. Indeed, it will help you not only clear your blocks about money, but in other areas of your life as well.

Chapter 4

MONEY AND RELATIONSHIPS

Four Great Ways to Talk About Money with Your "Inner Circle"

As mentioned, for many of us money and emotions often go hand in hand; in fact, arguments about money are one of the top three reasons for divorce. Money can affect our interactions with others in our inner circle as well, so if you have worked on the first three chapters and done the exercises, focusing on your relationships is the next logical step.

Our close relationships can be a safe place or a nightmare, and communication, or lack thereof, usually determines whether it is one or the other. The good news is we can improve our communication skills. In this chapter, we'll explore four straightforward ways to discuss money with the people who mean the most to us.

Step 1: Coming Clean

Let's start by being honest with our nearest and dearest about the state of our finances and our habits around money. This happens a lot less often than you might think. For example, people who are dating eventually discuss whether they want kids or not; they also talk about where they would like to live. However, not a lot of people talk about finances.

Why is this? Well, for one, it's not terribly romantic. Also, some people have been raised to believe that talking about one's finances is crude. They don't realize that money – and our approach to handling it – is far too important to ignore; in fact, the ultimate success of the relationship may depend upon it. Here are a few open questions to get the conversation started. Consider answering them yourself first so you have a better understanding of where you stand in these situations before engaging the other person.

Question1.: If you won the lottery and received three million dollars, what would you do with it?

_____

_____

_____

_____

_____

_____

_____

_____

_____

_____

_____

_____

_____

1(a). This above question can tell you a lot about a person's relationship to money. If you posed this question to your significant other and the reply was, "I would probably give it all away," how would you feel about that?

_____

_____

_____

_____

_____

_____

_____

_____

_____

_____

_____

_____

_____

_____

_____

_____

1(b). What if the response was, "I would not tell anybody and immediately put it into stocks"? How would you feel about that?

_____

_____

_____

_____

_____

_____

_____

_____

_____

_____

_____

_____

_____

_____

_____

1(c). Another response might be, "Oh, I don't know, I would figure it out if and when it happened to me." Is there a feeling you get from that response?

_____

_____

_____

_____

_____

_____

_____

_____

_____

_____

_____

_____

There are no right or wrong responses here – all of them are valid. The question is, which are a good match for you? If you and your love are on the same page, the flow of the relationship will be a lot smoother. If you know you are emotional when it comes to finances, working through these responses will give you a better understanding of how you might react and give you a chance to explore your viewpoints more in detail. Ask why you feel the way you do and keep digging. When you get to the reason that feels less emotion-based, you are ready to have this conversation with your significant other or anyone in your inner circle.

Question 2: Are you a spender, or a saver?

_____

_____

_____

_____

_____

_____

_____

_____

_____

_____

_____

_____

_____

_____

_____

_____

_____

_____

This is an important question to ask. Again, there is no right or wrong answer, but knowing how your partner works with money can help you identify potential relationship issues.

Find some time to look at how you two will work with money as a couple. If one is a spender and the other needs to have some savings in order to feel comfortable, this is an opportunity to have a larger conversation about finances.

There are many ways to negotiate this issue. For example, you might have separate accounts for spending, household bills, and savings. You might also place the partner for whom savings is important in charge of those savings.

Remember, it is important for each person to have what they feel they need, so get creative. For example, you might open separate savings accounts for "big dreams" such as homes or vacations, and/or use the "envelope method" for your spending money – once the cash is gone, that is it for the month. This helps you get a grounded idea of what is financially doable and what is not, especially if you are more of a visual person.

Question 3: If we find ourselves deep in debt, how will we get out of it?

_____

_____

_____

_____

_____

_____

_____

_____

_____

_____

_____

_____

_____

_____

Now more than ever, people are coming out of school with significant debt. How you manage that debt impacts you both individually and as part of a couple. In other words, you and your significant other must be on the same page as to how you are going to pay these debts down. Discuss them as a team and consult with financial professionals as needed (see Chapter 8). If you do this, even seemingly insurmountable mountains of debt can be conquered. Again, the key is to tackle it together, which brings us to Step 2.

Step 2: Shared ownership of financial matters

As you can tell by now, the saying "United we stand, divided we fall" can also apply to your inner circle, specifically your partner, when it comes to financial matters. If you have asked all your questions and determined that you and your closest peeps are a good financial match, you may be ready to take the next step, which is deciding whether to commit to shared ownership of all financial matters moving forward or keep them separate.

If you decide to share the bank accounts, be sure that each partner is clear on these four points:

1. Decide on an amount of money that *neither of you* can spend without talking to the other partner first.

This amount is going to be wildly different for everyone, so it is a meaningful conversation to have. The best way to arrive at an amount is to have a budget meeting and figure out how much cash you have not already dedicated to bills. Next, be honest about what a big purchase item is for each of you. A fun way to do this is to have each person write down an amount that they consider a big purchase, then take turns revealing the number and why it was picked. You may be surprised to know how many times this amount is tied to an emotional memory. Now, if you've chosen similar amounts, great; if, on the other hand, they are far apart, you will need to do some negotiating. This process creates trust, so it is essential that both partners agree to honor whatever amount you decide upon.

2. Decide the best person to pay the bills and be the general keeper of the balance sheet. If it's unclear who should do this, switch off for a couple of months and see who is the best fit. This is not a judgment of either person; some people are just more comfortable with finances and time-sensitive tasks.

3. Discuss and agree upon how you will allocate your money each month. How much spendable income will be shared? How much gets put into savings? This task is going to be fluid because bills can change and unexpected expenditures come up. Again, regular communication is what will make or break this plan.

4. Is there high-interest debt that needs to be paid down quickly?

That is part of the conversation as well. Each person in the relationship needs to be very honest about the debt they are carrying.

This needs to be a no-judgment conversation – remember, we are looking for solutions here, not accusations. That said, shame is often wrapped up in debt, which can stir up defensive emotions rather quickly.

In this case, it may be a good idea to bring in an objective third party who both of you agree will be part of your personal finance team. In the last chapter of this book, I will discuss the people you may want to consider for this role.

There are many resources to assist with the elimination of debt, but it all starts with you. The goal must come from an inner desire to be in a different space financially – that is, one of abundance and releasing the thought of lack.

Step 3: Have a "Money Safety Net" for the Household

If you have listened to any major money guru you have heard this piece of advice before. We know it is just good common sense to have a household safety net; we may even make a plan, vow, or New Year's resolution to build one, yet all too often we keep putting off saving until next month, then the month after, as life and other expenses get in the way. In case you have never heard about this before, the idea is to save three months of income that will be there to protect you if anything unexpected happens.

The money needs to be a savings account that you can access at a moment's notice, and there is the rub. Oftentimes we dip into our savings not because there is an emergency, but because we feel lack and try to quell that feeling by buying something for ourselves. Familiar, right? The truth is, this is a habit that, like any other, can be shifted. Here are some ideas to help you build and maintain a savings account that really will be a safety net.

1. Have more than one savings account. You can have as many as you want! Decide what you need extra cash for and create a savings account for each of those larger cash outlays (i.e. a Christmas account or accounts for a new car or wardrobe), then set it up so a predetermined amount from your paycheck(s) is automatically placed in those accounts. As you watch them build, so will your excitement, and the feeling of empowerment that you are able to save toward a goal. This will help you keep saving until you have reached your magical number, and perhaps beyond it.

You might also be able to set up a savings account through your work – a 401(k), perhaps, or a Roth IRA. Just remember that these types of accounts are for long-term plans, usually those you're making for your retirement.

2. Put the savings account in the "saver's" name. As mentioned earlier, it's important to know who the spender in the family is and who is the saver. The saver is usually the person who feels safer if there is a "stash" of money somewhere and is therefore motivated to keep that money in the emergency account. So while you might have money from both partners' paychecks automatically deposited into savings, only the saver will be able to access it if an emergency arises.

Remember, this is not about judgment, just an acknowledgment that people have different perspectives on money. One person may want the security of having extra cash and the other may not have that emotional need.

3. Another possibility is to automatically send a portion of each paycheck into your savings account(s). For many of us, it's less distressing if the money goes directly into savings, rather than having it in our checking account first and then seeing it moved out. If you're one of these people, consider setting up these automatic deposits (or ask your banker for assistance). Over time, you will not miss the money in your daily life and your savings will start to build.

4. Create a "me" savings account. Each time you choose not to spend money on a discretionary purchase, that amount goes into the "me" savings account. Think about how many times you buy a coffee during the month. What if you decided to put that money into a "me" account instead? How quickly would that add up? This practice builds healthy saving habits and can even make it fun!

Step 4: Commit to a Long-Term Team Saving Approach

Long-term savings is a must for all of us – we cannot rely on Social Security to be enough to live on when we retire. Again, this book is not about setting up those systems, it is about getting in a place emotionally and mentally where you are excited to have a retirement account. Sadly, many of us think we must have a vast amount of money going towards this account. The thought is so defeating that we never even investigate what it would actually take.

Let's think about this from a different perspective. Even if you do not plan on retiring early (or not at all), wouldn't you like to have more discretion as to when and where you work? If so, a retirement income of any kind will give you more options. How freeing would that feel? Do you have a hobby you would like to turn into a moneymaker? Would having a retirement account to draw on make taking that leap easier? Do you want to be able to take a hiatus from your job to travel? Would having a nest egg make that a possibility? Having this account allows you to dream and keep the possibility of new horizons alive.

A retirement savings account such as a Roth IRA or a 401K is easy to set up. All it takes is a conversation with a financial advisor; you may even be able to talk to your banker about the options. You can start with a small amount of money each month – perhaps twenty dollars (or three coffee house coffees). The key is to start simply. No matter how old or young you are, just take that first step and get into the habit of putting money in a long-term account.

Again, think of this as your "dreams" or "freedom" account. Give it a name that makes you smile and feel as if you are valuing yourself and taking care of yourself in the best possible way. You are saying to yourself, "I believe in my dreams enough to invest in them." There is no greater act of self-love than that.

Do your research. Ask friends and others you trust for advice on what firm to go with and how to invest. It's also important to know yourself and be honest about identifying your emotions and what you are comfortable with financially. Are you a risk-taker, conservative, or somewhere in-between? Also, make sure the company you invest with is one you can trust, and that you like the person you will be communicating with about your retirement fund. The company needs to be a feel-good place for you, so follow your gut and keep looking until you find a good match.

Remember, this is a long-term investment. That means you may not want to look at it every day, especially if it is in the stock market, with its normal (and sometimes dramatic fluctuations). Yes, the amount will go up and down, but over a long period it will (mostly) go up. Try to limit how often you review this account, perhaps once a month, or once every other month – especially if you are new to the market or not very comfortable with risk.

There are many calculators out there to help with your long-term savings, and how you can build and create a healthy nest egg. You can start with minimal monthly investments and end up with a significant amount of money over time. We'll discuss this more in Chapter 8.

What about the Kids?

Many people believe that you should not talk to children about money. They are concerned about stressing them out, or think that money is simply not a topic for children. Here is the reality: our kids are always watching us and learning from how we deal with life – including our finances. If we do not talk to them about how we make decisions involving money, they are going to draw their own conclusions and those ideas may color their relationship with money as adults.

Do you have a memory of your parents around money? Is it possible that the memory has influenced how you think about money or things that require a money exchange? It is not your parents' fault. Like most people, they were doing the best they could and were probably unaware of what they said regarding money.

Let's start with something many of us heard as kids and might say more often than we realize: "We can't afford that." Stop and think for a minute – are those words really true? Now try saying this and see how it feels: "We are choosing to pay for_____
instead of getting _____."
Do you see how that changes the energy around that choice?

Phrasing things this way also makes things clearer for your children. It helps them to understand how money moves and that we need to direct the flow.

Pay attention to the language you use when speaking about money, as this is an indicator of your energy around it. Here's an example:

Try being thankful that you can pay whatever bills you are able to pay. So many of us tighten up and have negative energy when we see or think about our bills, and our kids can feel that. Our response makes them shy away from anything having to do with money and bills; they may avoid paying bills as adults, even if they have the money. (This behavior is more common than you may think!) Being aware of our feelings when we are moving money (whether receiving or giving it), will help everyone in the family, especially the kids.

Paying bills is also an opportunity to explain finances to our kids; for example, by telling them that the way we live requires us to share our money with companies and people that assist us in having that lifestyle. For instance, we like being cool in the summer, right? Air conditioning uses electricity, and the electric company provides us electricity to use in our home in exchange for some of our money. You might be surprised at how many kids have no idea that you must pay for these things. Knowledge is power, and knowing where the money goes and why will help your kids have a deeper understanding of the choices that you make.

Here are some quick ideas for teaching kids about money by age group.

Age 2 and up: You can start using this as soon as your child can ask for a toy in a store. Remember the scavenger hunt exercise? Have one now, by having your kids search for coins in clothes, in or under the couch, and so on. Each time they find a coin, have them put it in a jar. These coins are their money. Once the jar is filled, take it to a bank or a coin star and turn the coins into dollar bills. Make sure the money is one-dollar bills, so it is easier for them to visualize how much the things they want cost.

Next, go to the toy aisle and allow your child to pick a toy. Show your child how much the toy would cost with the dollar bills. How much would be left to save for the next time? This activity is a great way to see what kind of natural spender or saver your child is.

I did this with my son, and we spent twenty minutes in the toy aisle while he looked at everything and compared the prices to how many dollar bills he had. My son is a natural saver; he likes to have money in the bank. Other kids are natural spenders; they do not care if there is any money left over or not. Knowing this will help you guide your children as they learn to navigate how they will work with money throughout their lives.

Ages 8 and up: Open a savings account that is just for them. Banks LOVE it when children open savings accounts. Many times, they give the child a goody bag with toys and gifts to encourage saving. They know that if a child starts saving early and learns what it feels like to have money grow, they will develop good habits for a lifetime.

As the parent, your job is to set the terms and how your child is accountable for them. You'll need to decide how much money will go into that account every month and if your child will be required to do chores in exchange for it, as opposed to giving them an allowance free and clear. These decisions are not just about growing the savings account, but about your family community.

Regardless of how the money comes to be deposited, make sure deposits occur at least once a month. Why are regular deposits important? Because the excitement that is generated from seeing money grow will be a positive vibration that your child will remember. This positive feeling will then be linked with saving money and understanding how currency works. It might attach to growing an amount of money for bigger purchases or saved for emergencies so they can feel safe.

It is also interesting to see where a child's natural comfort point is with regard to the amount of money they have in their savings account. Once it gets to a certain point, say over one hundred dollars, allow them to take some of the money out to spend on a more expensive item. See if they are willing to do so or if they hesitate because it will mean having less in their account. Bring attention to the hesitation so they understand that there is an energy exchange that happens when we use money. The bigger the amount spent, the more we will feel it.

You might also decide to talk about buyer's remorse – the feeling we get when something we thought we wanted is not all it's cracked up to be and we realize we'd rather have our money back. It is another opportunity to teach and guide your kids about dealing with money and the emotions it may bring up for them.

Final age group, 13 and up: If you have engaged in these activities and feel your child is ready to take on more responsibility, perhaps it is time to add a checking account and debit card to the mix.

For a lot of parents, this is a scary thought, and here is what I tell them: you can do this now, while they are still under your roof where you can guide them, or you can wait and have them thrown into the deep end of the pool once they are out on their own. Which one sounds better? Most agree they should try this out now so their kids can make smaller mistakes and learn from them to build better money habits.

Most banks will allow a thirteen- or fourteen-year-old to have a checking account if it is attached to the parents' account. This is safe, because you have already gotten into the habit of checking your account daily and now you can check your child's activity as well. Perhaps it is something you can do together to build solid positive habits around money.

There are two important skills children will learn from having a checking account – taking care of a debit card and keeping track of their spending habits – both of which are key to handling money successfully once they go out on their own. Again, you will need to decide as a family what will happen if the debit card is lost, or if they spend all the money in their account, et cetera. Work with your banker to put limits on spending and blocks when the amount goes down to a certain amount. Another approach is to allow your child to find themselves in that situation. Together you can work on solutions that will get your children out of the trouble, and a plan for what to do so it doesn't happen again in the future.

There are now apps for kids to work with money, and they can be an awesome tool. Download one that you like and take some time to observe your child while using it. Are they a visual learner? If so, you may also want to start them off with the envelope system. As mentioned in a previous chapter, this involves putting cash into envelopes, usually once a month. This system works well for visual learners because once the cash is gone, there is no more spending until the time comes to refill the envelope. They can see how much cash they have during the month and be able to make choices on spending from this grounded space.

Using envelopes also helps the child be independent and helps the parent resist shaming. The child has natural consequences (an empty envelope) that they will need to work through on their own – a win/win in my book.

Is this a lot of work? Yes. Is it worth the effort? Absolutely! With you as their guide, your children will be empowered to make better money decisions – and go out into the world with a much better chance of creating a life and world they love! Start with the activity that is least intimidating for you and grow from there. The age guidelines are simply that, guidelines. You can start this money education at any time in your child's life. You got this!

Chapter 5

THE BAROMETER FOR MONEY CHOICES

Values and How They Help Us Choose

T hese days, values seem more important than ever. The interesting thing about values is that they all have equal weight on paper – they only take on a life of their own when you put your own meaning to the words. Do you know what values are most important to you, or have you mostly adopted those of others? To figure it out, let's start by comparing two values: acknowledgment and accomplishment. For some people they can mean almost the same thing; for others, they are very different. Take, for example, Moriah, a young instructor, and what these values mean to her.

Moriah is diligently working on a new class that will be running this weekend. She is nearly finished with all curriculum and other documents and is getting excited about it all coming together. However, alone with that excitement and anticipation are familiar feelings of fear and dread. The fear and dread are coming from Moriah's need for acknowledgment from an outside source – in this case, her boss. The need for acknowledgment from others has been a constant hurdle for Moriah for many years now.

This acknowledgment is an unknown value. She has not taught this class before and has no example to follow. For the first time in a long time, she feels like she is flying by the seat of her pants. Looking through her presentation, she again feels that rush of accomplishment; she also realizes that she would feel even better if her boss looked at the class and acknowledged all her hard work. She craves the validation of hearing that her work is excellent.

At the same time Moriah wonders why she values other people's opinions over her own. What does that say about how she values herself? Would it be possible, this one time, to recognize that she had done her research, put in the work to create a curriculum, and KNOW that this class will be well received? At that moment, Moriah makes the conscious choice to choose the value of accomplishment over acknowledgment by other people. She feels empowered and confident. She feels strong enough to be able to present to her students and know deep within that she is adding to their lives by providing the richness that is learning new things.

Here is the benefit of being aware of our values and examining them. Values help us make decisions based on what has meaning in our inner world. If we are true to that state, we can withstand any naysayers, doubts, or setbacks. If we make decisions based on our actual inner values, it empowers us rather than deflating and setting us on our heels.

Our values may change as we go through our lives; however, our most closely held values tend to hold steady. For example, according to "Generational Differences in the Workplace: Personal Values, Behaviors and Popular Beliefs,"[2] family security and health are the top two values that tend to stay true as we age and also maintain their internal value.

Interesting, right? I would have thought love would be on the list, or happiness, but they seem not to be as important as we age.

On the other hand, it's curious that most of what we see on the news, TV shows and movies does not reflect these values, but is about war and

---

[2] Gibson, J., Greenwood, R., Murphy, E. (2009). "Generational Beliefs: Personal Values, Behaviors and Popular Beliefs." https://clutejournals.com/index.php/JDM/article/view/4959/5051

fighting. If family security and health are important to us, many of us, in all generations currently living, why do we not see that reflected in the world? Where is the disconnected piece? Could it be inside our own minds? If that is so, what can we do to obtain the family security and health we desire within ourselves?

The big question for our purposes here is, how does this connect with "redefining rich"? As I said above, our inner worlds create our outer world. If we are not clear on what we value, and what we hold close to our hearts, we could be forever looking for that stability, safety, and health that we seek outside ourselves. True richness resides in our minds, our thoughts, and our hearts. These thoughts create or destroy our worlds and are found in the environment we manifest every day.

Let's look at this in another way. If we are clear on what we value, our decisions on how we use money and our other assets become a little easier to make.

Remember Henry from Chapter 1? He has been offered a job in another state, for a significant increase in income, but he was torn because he would have to move his family. Let's say instead that his family could stay put but the job would require Henry to travel a lot so he would have to be away from them for some time each month. While it would make his family financially secure, is it worth the sacrifice of time with his family? The answer to this question depends on Tom's strongest value. If that value is family security, then chances are he will try to make this new job work. The financial stability will assist his family in creating a happy home, especially if everyone in the family also holds family security as a top value.

Now, if the top value for Tom is balance, this may be a tougher call. Balance involves many aspects, including time spent at work and time spent with family and friends. If Tom will have to be in another place for the whole week and only have time with family and friends on weekends, this may feel out of balance. In this case, it might make more sense to find a side job or another way to earn more money. Or, Tom and his family might sit down and find a way to work with their finances to make his current salary go father.

So you see, Tom's top value(s) must be at the core of this decision on whether to take the job or not. If he goes against his values, he will eventually be unhappy and dissatisfied, no matter how much he earns.

Do you know what your top five values are? Remember, they may shift as you go through life, so it may be time to reassess. I invite you to take the time to work through this next tool. It may take some time, but it will be worth it.

Knowing your values will empower you in making decisions in life, both big and small, because we do so from a grounded place. Like Tom, if we are not living our values, our lives will not be all they can be, regardless of our income; however, if we stay true to our values, oftentimes the money will follow.

Find your Core Values

Below are two hundred and thirty personal core values. Take a deep breath to center and ground yourself; then as you go through the list, underline or highlight any word that causes a reaction in your body. You have been working with sensations for a while now, you know which ones to pay attention to. Once you have gone through the whole list and highlighted the words that speak to you, we will proceed to the next step.

Acceptance	Ambition	Boldness
Accomplishment	Amusement	Bravery
Accountability	Assertiveness	Brilliance
Accuracy	Attentive	Calm
Achievement	Awareness	Candor
Adaptability	Balance	Capable
Alertness	Beauty	Careful
Altruism		

Challenge	Devotion	Genius
Charity	Dignity	Giving
Cleanliness	Discipline	Goodness
Clear	Discovery	Grace
Clever	Drive	Gratitude
Comfort	Effectiveness	Greatness
Commitment	Efficiency	Growth
Common sense	Empathy	Happiness
Communication	Empower	Hard work
Community	Endurance	Harmony
Compassion	Energy	Health
Competence	Enjoyment	Honesty
Concentration	Enthusiasm	Honor
Candor	Equality	Hope
Connection	Ethical	Humility
Consciousness	Excellence	Imagination
Consistency	Experience	Improvement
Contentment	Exploration	Independence
Contribution	Expressive	Individuality
Control	Fairness	Innovation
Conviction	Family	Inquisitive
Cooperation	Famous	Insightful
Courage	Fearless	Inspiring
Courtesy	Feelings	Integrity
Creation	Ferocious	Intelligence
Credibility	Fidelity	Intensity
Curiosity	Focus	Intuitive
Decisive	Foresight	Irreverent
Decisiveness	Fortitude	Joy
Dedication	Freedom	Justice
Dependability	Friendship	Kindness
Determination	Fun	Knowledge
Development	Generosity	Lawful

Leadership	Recognition	Structure
Learning	Recreation	Success
Liberty	Reflective	Support
Logic	Respect	Surprise
Love	Responsibility	Sustainability
Loyalty	Restraint	Talent
Mastery	Results-oriented	Teamwork
Maturity	Reverence	Temperance
Meaning	Rigor	Thankful
Moderation	Risk	Thorough
Motivation	Satisfaction	Thoughtful
Openness	Security	Timeliness
Optimism	Self-reliance	Tolerance
Order	Selfless	Toughness
Organization	Sensitivity	Traditional
Originality	Serenity	Tranquility
Passion	Service	Transparency
Patience	Sharing	Trust
Peace	Significance	Trustworthy
Performance	Silence	Truth
Persistence	Simplicity	Understanding
Playfulness	Sincerity	Uniqueness
Poise	Skill	Unity
Potential	Skillfulness	Valor
Power	Smart	Victory
Present	Solitude	Vigor
Productivity	Spirit	Vision
Professionalism	Spirituality	Vitality
Prosperity	Spontaneous	Wealth
Purpose	Stability	Welcoming
Quality	Status	Winning
Realistic	Stewardship	Wisdom
Reason	Strength	Wonder

2. Now, go back through the ones you underlined and highlighted and try to hone it down to your top ten. Take your time with this. Really tune in to your body and work with the sensations you feel as you read the words you chose. This is an opportunity for you to find your "yes" sensation. It is unique to each person, and it will be strong. It may take some patience as you create a way to get your values down to the top ten, but you can do it!

If you would like more guidance, try this:

1. Write down all the words you chose in two columns, in no particular order.

2. Once this is complete, start at the top of the list. Put your hands out palms up and imagine a word from one column in one hand and a word from the other column in the other hand.

3. Close your eyes and feel what is there. The word that feels lighter is the one that is chosen.

4. Write down or circle the word that felt lighter.

5. Go to the next row and repeat, continue until you have done this with all your words.

6. If the resulting word count is more than ten words, repeat this exercise again until you get it down to ten.

Next, write down the first word on your list and journal about what this word means to you. You can look up the definition if it helps, and it will be more meaningful if you wrote why you are attracted to this word. Repeat this process until you have done it for all ten words.

1. _____

_____

_____

_____

_____

_____

_____

_____

_____

_____

2. _____

_____

_____

_____

_____

_____

_____

_____

_____

_____

3. _____

_____

_____

_____

_____

_____

_____

_____

_____

_____

4. _____

_____

_____

_____

_____

_____

_____

_____

_____

_____

5. _____

_____

_____

_____

_____

_____

_____

_____

_____

_____

_____

6. _____

_____

_____

_____

_____

_____

_____

_____

_____

_____

_____

7. _____

_____

_____

_____

_____

_____

_____

_____

_____

_____

_____

8. _____

_____

_____

_____

_____

_____

_____

_____

_____

_____

_____

9. _____

_____

_____

_____

_____

_____

_____

_____

_____

_____

10. _____

_____

_____

_____

_____

_____

_____

_____

_____

_____

As you were writing out your words' meanings, did one or two really flow easily or raise emotion for you? If so, these are your top values. Reread and determine if what you felt the first time while writing out the meaning holds true.

Top 2 Values

_____

_____

_____

_____

_____

_____

_____

_____

_____

_____

_____

_____

_____

Consider keeping these two values in a place where you can pull them out whenever you need to be reminded of this exercise. It can be on a piece of paper or perhaps in the note section of your phone.

The next time you have a difficult decision to make regarding finances, remind yourself of these values.

I use this one often. For example, my spending temptation is self-improvement courses. I would love to be taking courses to understand myself and others every day of the week. However, these courses are an expenditure, so making the decision requires me to balance my two top values: curiosity and peace.

The first step is to take a closer look at the course. Is it a financial stretch for me, and if so, is it worth it? This question is easier to answer now that I am solid in my values. The stretch will be worth it if the course gives me knowledge I do not have, as it will satisfy my curiosity and I can use this new knowledge and/or skill to better myself and others. Seems like a no-brainer, right?

Not necessarily, because I have to look at my other top value: peace of mind. This value makes me think of what my top goals are currently. These goals have recently shifted, and as a result financial peace of mind has become key. It holds sway over all my other values. I can wait for this class until I have raised the extra money, knowing that will probably still be available.

What I notice about this process is it often takes away any reactive emotions. Because I chose these values and look at the issue using them as a lens, it takes away the sting of not taking the course at this time. For me, the short-term sacrifice is worth it.

Values keep us in a place of solid knowing of self. This can help us feel safe even when the ground under our feet starts to shift. You pick the values that have the most meaning for you. None are better or worse, yours are just right for you and mine are just right for me. Values are a great way to get to know yourself and, in the process, make those decisions that may take you out of your comfort zone. This exercise may take some time to complete, but it is so worth it. It also may be a tool you want to revisit as your life evolves and changes. Some values will remain, but many may change as your life circumstances change. If you are on the edge of a big change in your life, you may want to consider revisiting your values and see if there is a shift there as well.

Chapter 6

MONEY MONSTERS

The Nitty Gritty of Money Beliefs that May Not Be Serving You

Many of us think of money as a living thing. We may argue that we do not, but we do.

If we did not think of it in such a way, it would not take up so much of our inner thought time. Everyone has habits when it comes to money, and examining our thoughts about it can tell us a lot about where those habits stem from.

When I feel I have plenty of money, there is a sense of space and calm. All is well; there is enough for everything and everyone. It's when I feel that I do *not* have enough money that things get interesting. I feel restricted, which makes me grumpy or bitter. Suddenly, I feel like I NEED all sorts of stuff I did not need before. I have stress and anxiety about paying bills and sustaining my lifestyle.

Mind you, nothing has really changed in my world during these times. I still have my job and my spouse has his. There will be more paychecks coming in, the bills will get paid and yet, the feeling of restriction and lack is there. What monster is this? Clearly, it is not the money itself, and it is not that I NEED anything. All my basic needs are and always have been met. The monster, therefore, must reside in my thoughts and feelings, but what is causing them?

Many people deal with these monsters. Most are not conscious of it being separate from money, and so money and the people with money get blamed. How much negative thought and energy have been thrown toward the one-percenters in the past few years? Our frustration with not having gets morphed into the idea that others have too much, and it is not fair! Suddenly, we are back in elementary school and someone got more of a treat than we did. What is the truth? Is there only so much money to go around, or is that merely a perception?

Here is a "money monster" thoughts list:

There is never enough.

I can remember feeling this way. It was such a heavy and uncomfortable thought that it colored everything I did and everything I saw. This thought made me overly sensitive to those I perceived had more. I wanted to be angry with them. I wanted to tell them life is not fair, and that it's unfair that it is so easy for them to have all they need and so hard for me. This way of thinking was getting me nowhere fast. I had to turn it around, and I did so by changing the words I used. I started saying, "There is always enough." This simple, one-word change in that phrase began to change everything for me; it shifted my perspective on what I wanted and that new perspective became my truth.

By saying I always have enough, I started to see the many ways I already had enough, usually more than enough. And, as a result, I began to attract more. It seemed like magic at the time, and maybe it was. It was the start of my magical journey into abundance.

Gratitude is such a powerful practice; when I get to a place of lack it is always the first place I look. On the other hand, everytime I have let the practice slip, in creeps the negative thoughts and a lack attitude. The words in red need to be inserted into this sentence.

Do you find yourself thinking there is never enough? If so, simple gratitude practices will help you turn things around. It can be as simple as waking up and thinking of three things you are grateful for – for example, I am grateful for my breath; I am grateful for the pillow under my head;

I am grateful for the beautiful air all around me. Try this practice every morning as soon as you open your eyes. If this is a new habit for you, give yourself something you will see first thing in the morning to remind you of this practice. Give it a try – I know you will be glad you did!

You can also start your own gratitude practice. What is a plan that will work for you? Would you be willing to write down the plan here? This will help you commit to a gratitude practice.

_____

_____

_____

_____

_____

_____

_____

_____

_____

_____

_____

_____

_____

_____

_____

All I need is a million dollars and then I would be set.

I hear this idea all the time – not just from my friends, but from people in my classes and even people I pass on the street or in the aisle of a store. Is this the truth? Would having a million dollars set me up for no more problems and no more worries? (Remember when we broke down the interest from a million dollars earlier in the book.) We hear stories of people getting these windfalls and their lives changing for the worst. Try asking a few of your friends if they have ever known anyone who inherited or received a million dollars or more. Usually, you will find at least one person who knows someone who received a large sum of money.

When I ask this question, I usually hear stories of people who inherited money and lost it all or won a sum of money and spent it all or gave it away. Why is that? What is it about money that creates so many strong and hidden emotions in people? What makes the emotional pendulum swing from joy and ecstasy of receiving to sorrow and anger from letting it slip away, in many cases within six months? It all comes down to your thoughts and beliefs. If you are thinking, "I want more money" but you believe a large amount of money seems to bring trouble, therein lies the energetic rub. If this thought pattern hits home for you, below is some space to journal around the statement, "A large sum of money brings trouble." Examine for yourself if that is a true statement or an emotional response made from past experiences or observations of people who have had trouble with a windfall of money.

_____

_____

_____

_____

_____

_____

_____

_____

_____

_____

_____

If I take the emotion out of the equation, and if I step back and look at a million dollars with clear eyes, I can see the money for what it is – simply a tool I need to learn how to use, rather than an end-all, be-all that will make all my wishes come true.

Try this for yourself. In the space below, write down ideas on how you can become stronger in the belief that money is simply a tool. What would be a good first step for you? How can you bring this awareness of emotional charges around money forward to your conscious mind?

_____

_____

_____

_____

_____

_____

_____

_____

_____

_____

_____

_____

_____

_____

Here are a few more common "money monster" thoughts to explore. I invite you to journal your thoughts on these as well. Explore how these thoughts hit you; what are the sensations?

The people with top incomes need to give more because others don't have enough.

As mentioned, I have struggled with this one mightily, and here is what I have come to understand. When I think or say this, I am, in effect, pointing a finger at someone else. It also implies that there is a finite sum of money to go around. Again, money is just a tool that we make more of when we need to. Are you aware that the government prints money when they need to? Is it to an extreme? No, there are checks and balances involved, but the bottom line is there is always more where that came from. So, if that is true, then I need to think about how I am working with money and how I am using it. If I need more, how can I acquire more income? Do I have thoughts that are stopping me or giving me excuses to not strive for more?

_____

_____

_____

_____

_____

_____

_____

_____

_____

_____

_____

_____

_____

_____

Rich people are greedy.

This is an interesting one. The first time you heard this or had this thought, what was happening? In my case, I had asked someone I knew had plenty of money to give me a loan. They said no, and in my mind I accused them, and others like them, of being greedy. Now I know that this was not accurate.

Why did they say no? Well, at the time I asked for the loan I was not being a responsible steward of money. They had been watching me and knew that if I got that loan I would go through that money and not be able to pay them back. Moreover, the bad feelings (mostly my guilt) that resulted from this would probably ruin our relationship. In essence, their "no" was telling me that they valued the relationship more than the money. I will say it again, they valued the relationship more than the money. Tough thought to take in, but true. What about you? Have you ever had the "rich people are greedy" thought? Here is a place to work through that thought.

_____

_____

_____

_____

_____

_____

_____

_____

_____

_____

_____

_____

_____

Rich people are penny pinchers.

This one makes me giggle a little. I had this thought when watching my elders clipping coupons when I knew they had more than enough to get anything they wanted. What I did not understand at the time is the joy that comes with being a good steward of the abundance you are given.

My grandma loved clipping coupons. For her, it was a kind of game called "How much money can I save at the grocery store?" It gave her joy. That said, she had also grown up during the Depression and understood what it was to barely (and I mean *barely*) get by. Because of what she went through, she learned to use everything she had and to get every drop out of anything around her. What's interesting is that "minimalism" has now become a popular trend. For my grandma, there was no choice, it was a way of survival, and it shaped how she dealt with money the rest of her life.

A great side benefit is that her family's savings account grew, which brought her a feeling of safety she hadn't had during her youth. This is why she was able to see clipping coupons as a game. It is all in the attitude. I am working every day on being a better steward of my money. Where is my attitude? Am I able to find joy in less? Is there a kind of elegance in crafting a life with less stuff? Maybe my grandma had a secret that not a lot of people know. Less stuff to take care of is freeing and money needs to be taken care of and treated with respect. What do you think?

Is this a money monster (belief) that needs to be examined by you? What would it take to become a better steward of money or let go of the idea that rich people are penny-pinchers?

_____

_____

_____

_____

_____

_____

_____

_____

_____

_____

_____

_____

_____

I take care of others, even when it's difficult. I am generous to others; I always help.

This is a tough one for me. It has a ton of emotionally charged triggers attached to it. This is where I must look at how I attached my worth to how others perceive me. It has been important to me in the past to have people like me and think well of me – even people I don't really know all that well.

It's funny, as I am writing this, I am getting that familiar feeling in my heart and my stomach. This feeling happens when I am doing something I am afraid of, like the example of the little boy in the first chapter who is going to school on the first day of kindergarten. The phrasing, "I always help, even when it is difficult," runs deep for me. It goes back to when I was young and watched others be judged for their actions in many different social situations.

As someone who has always been in a "helping" profession, I fell into the idea that I "should" help everyone, regardless of the cost to me. Now I understand that the idea of helping everyone regardless of cost is called martyrdom. I used to like the idea of being a martyr, if I am telling the deep-down truth, but not any longer.

Here is what I understand now. If I martyr myself for others, I am diminishing the good I can do for them. When I am giving from a place anything other than abundance, I am taking the chance of becoming bitter and blaming my bitterness on others. The bitterness is brought on by not taking care of myself. This is true for me in both how I spend my time and how much I charge others for that time and for my skills. For many years, I worked and over-gave to the point of exhaustion. This played out in lower income and a lot of bitterness and blaming of others for not valuing me. Here is the painful bottom line: if I don't value myself, no one else will.

So, let's take this to the money arena. If I give discounts for my services or I give others money when I don't have the money I need to cover my needs, is that really helping either of us? No, because now I am struggling and bitter and feeling anxious about where I am financially and find myself working even harder to just get by. As I am doing this, how easy is it for me to judge what they do with the money I gave them? This is part of the bitterness, and it can ruin the relationship with the person the money was given to.

Here is another way. I concentrate on filling my own cup first. I set my prices so I can give and receive compensation that will fill my cup. The more compensation, the faster the cup is filled. This gives me time to take care of myself and fill my cup even more. When someone asks for my financial help, I tell the truth: I am still working on taking care of myself. There is no shame in this. In the long run I am doing the person who asked for a discount or a loan a favor. If I gave to them when I was still in need or my cup was not filled, it would end in bitterness and per-haps the end of a relationship. This is something I am no longer willing to do. I need to fill my cup first and keep it filled. When it runs over into the saucer, then I can give from an open heart, with an open hand – no bitterness involved.

As you can see, I am still a work in progress on this one. How about you? Here is some space to start exploring that. Note: It's a tough one, so take your time and be kind to yourself.

_____

_____

_____

_____

_____

_____

_____

_____

_____

_____

_____

_____

_____

_____

_____

This list is just the tip of the iceberg. There are so many thoughts that enter our minds when it comes to money and the use of it. Here is a space to write down your own money monster thoughts, and you can come back to it whenever you feel you have mastered the others. The more we work to bring forward these hidden beliefs and debunk them, the better we are at working with money and wealth as simply a tool to get us where we want to go. Remember, work on these when your cup is full, and you can dig in without shaming yourself. You are doing big work on yourself, so be kind.

Here is the space for your money monster list:

_____

_____

_____

_____

_____

_____

_____

_____

_____

_____

_____

_____

_____

_____

_____

_____

When I read about or talk to people who manage money well, I realize that they do not equate money with emotion. There is never a thought that there is not enough, or that they cannot do this because they will seem greedy. Money is simply a means of exchange, and because of this their emotions do not stop them from making decisions that would work for the best interest of their project or business.

That said, just because they know emotions and money do not mix does not mean they don't find themselves in that trap at times. This is why even the most successful people work with trusted advisors. They have learned to recognize when their emotions have taken over and that is when they reach out for help. Someone who lives outside these emotions can be the voice of reason or able to see a different perspective.

In Chapter 8 you will find a list of ways to create a financial team. These will be the people who can advise you when emotions overwhelm the ability to think through a financial decision clearly. Remember in Chapter 1 when you started thinking about the people in your life who handle money in a way you admire. This list is the start of your financial team. Keep in mind that they might not be related to you or even have known you for very long; what's important is that they can tell you hard truths and you will be able to listen to what they have to say. Seek out those that you admire and would be able to listen to even when you are in the throes of being in a highly emotional state (i.e. fearful, ashamed, et cetera).

These people will be worth their weight in gold. Start looking for them now, and you may be surprised by who you find.

Here is a space to start a list of potential people for your financial team. Note: some of these people will be mentors and some will be paid for their services. All have a place on this list.

_____

_____

_____

_____

_____

_____

_____

_____

_____

_____

_____

_____

_____

_____

Chapter 7

VISUALLY DEFINING YOUR RICH

Putting All the New Concepts in One Place

Whew!

These exercises can lead to major shifts in thinking and in action. Now it feels like it is time to do something fun. Do you agree? Good!

This activity is a version of a vision board.

If you've never heard of them, a vision board is a visual representation of what we want in life. I have seen vision boards with favorite quotes, pictures, or a combination of both and perhaps a trinket too. You can even create them on the computer or your phone! Vision boards can be any size, and any configuration if it speaks to what you desire.

Why is this important to do? Well, most people are very visual; moreover, our subconscious mind works in pictures. Our senses (especially sight and smells) bring forth the strongest memories, and that is what our subconscious uses to help us make decisions that will keep us safe. See how that works? If our memories are not serving our current reality, that can be a problem. A vision board is one way to create new visions that can then allow our subconscious mind to embrace the reality we truly want to live. Besides, it is creative and fun!

Step 1:

Think about all the different pieces of your life that will assist you in creating your *rich life.* Some of these pieces will be in great shape! Fantastic! Find an image that matches the feeling that you have in that area of your life. In other categories, however, you may still have work to do. That's fantastic too! Why? Because now you get to use your imagination to create the ultimate feeling you want in each category. Your imagination is where the vision board really does its magic, because it will assist you in looking at what you want rather than what you do not want.

Below are some ideas of categories you could use. This is by no means an exhaustive list, but it's enough to get you going and fire up those creative juices. Feel free to add any categories that will help you visualize the life you desire.

In each category write out your wildest fantasy of what this specific part of your life would look like if there were no limits. You do not have to use every category I've listed here. In fact, choose the ones that are the most important to you. Focus on the ones that help you feel that you are living a rich, abundant, and wealthy life.

Some categories may include the following:

- Health

  This is considered to be the greatest form of wealth. If I am healthy, I can do what I want in life unencumbered by the needs that can come with illness or fatigue. Take a close look at your motivation when it comes to health. Do you want to lose weight because it will help you be healthier, or because you will look better? This is not a judgment, but a way to figure out what visuals you may use when it comes to this category on your vision board.

_____

_____

_____

_____

_____

_____

_____

_____

_____

_____

_____

_____

_____

_____

_____

_____

_____

- Mental Health

  More recently, this category has been emphasized as an important quality of life topic. Are there some new habits you want to acquire that speak to mental health and your ability to roll with difficult life circumstances? What habits that appeal to you would go in this category?

  _____

  _____

  _____

  _____

  _____

  _____

  _____

  _____

  _____

  _____

  _____

  _____

  _____

  _____

  _____

  _____

  _____

  _____

- Relationships with family and friends and/or community.

  This one could be great for you, or it may need some work. It is up to you to rate whether you need more time with these people or want a specific type of get-together to develop. What are your needs in this category and are they being met? If not, what would get those needs a bit closer to being met?

  _____

  _____

  _____

  _____

  _____

  _____

  _____

  _____

  _____

  _____

  _____

  _____

  _____

  _____

  _____

  _____

  _____

  _____

- Career

  Whether you are just starting out or are ready to make a major shift, this can be an interesting category. What are your dreams when it comes to your career?

  _____

  _____

  _____

  _____

  _____

  _____

  _____

  _____

  _____

  _____

  _____

  _____

  _____

  _____

  _____

  _____

  _____

  _____

- Mastermind groups (a community that assists with your work or career)

This category comes in handy, especially if you are working from home and the lack of social interaction becomes a challenge. Mastermind groups are a great support if you are the kind of person who works best when you can talk to others about your ideas. Would you be interested in forming a mastermind group? If you are, what would it look like?

_____

_____

_____

_____

_____

_____

_____

_____

_____

_____

_____

_____

_____

_____

_____

- Fun

  This category is important, especially if you are a hard-driving person and always striving for more. Our minds need downtime and creative time in order to rejuvenate and be more productive. What do you do for fun? Are there enough fun activities in your life? How can you create more fun?

  _____

  _____

  _____

  _____

  _____

  _____

  _____

  _____

  _____

  _____

  _____

  _____

  _____

  _____

  _____

  _____

  _____

- Spiritual

  This category is for practices or interactions that assist you with getting to know your higher self, God, the Universe, and so on, so clearly it is very broad, with many different applications. Whatever is right for you is perfect. Is this something you want more of in your rich life? What would bring in more spiritual understanding?

  _____

  _____

  _____

  _____

  _____

  _____

  _____

  _____

  _____

  _____

  _____

  _____

  _____

  _____

  _____

  _____

  _____

  _____

- Love/romance

    What characteristics make the person you would like to be with? What do they look like? What do they like to do? What are the quirks that you would find adorable? These are just starting points, feel free to go from there.

    _____

    _____

    _____

    _____

    _____

    _____

    _____

    _____

    _____

    _____

    _____

    _____

    _____

    _____

    _____

    _____

    _____

    _____

- Living environment

  This can be the type of home you want to live in (i.e. its style and color palette, et cetera), as well as the part of the world you would like to live in. Do you want to live in the country, the city, downtown? There are so many choices, so much to think about.

  _____

  _____

  _____

  _____

  _____

  _____

  _____

  _____

  _____

  _____

  _____

  _____

  _____

  _____

  _____

  _____

  _____

  _____

- Travel

  This is an exciting category, so let your mind go wild. What places do you want to see and experience? Now it is even possible to go to outer space! What is interesting to you?

  _____

  _____

  _____

  _____

  _____

  _____

  _____

  _____

  _____

  _____

  _____

  _____

  _____

  _____

  _____

  _____

  _____

  _____

- Experiences you want to have

  Skydiving, hiking the Pacific Crest Trail, kayaking your favorite river, learning to play an instrument, taking a class – the list is never-ending. What experiences do you want to have? Try out thinking about an experience and see how your body responds. If it makes you tingle, write it down!

- **Add more categories here**
- **Category:** _____

_____

_____

_____

_____

_____

_____

_____

_____

_____

- **Category:** _____

_____

_____

_____

_____

_____

_____

_____

_____

_____

Remember, this is your rich life, filled with wealth and abundance *of all kinds.*

Some of these categories may already be rich for you. If so, use them. When you are thinking about it, how do you feel physically? Do you feel all tingly, or is there a lighter feel or a warm glow? That is your marker for the other categories. Keep going until you get a similar feeling in your body for each category you selected.

This is your vision board, and you get to choose how many categories you desire; that said, I suggest that you try to keep it to no more than four categories as this will help your mind to focus. If you feel you are in a good flow, you may consider creating your vision board from a corkboard or other medium that is easy to change as we accomplish these new visions. This may also help those who are hesitant to try because they want it to be perfect. If it is a corkboard, then it can be changed on a whim, so each day is a new opportunity to add to this vision as it becomes clearer.

Be kind to yourself and take your time. This process is like peeling the layers of an onion. Start with the categories that seem easier and then move on to the others as you are ready.

Step 2:

Ideas for ways to create your vision board:

- Buy a corkboard.

  This board can be powerful because you can change it whenever you want! Corkboard is easy to attach 3D items like tokens or charms. Start collecting anything and everything that speaks to the goals you have created in the journaling piece in Step 1.
- Go old school with a posterboard!

  Just cutting and pasting, creating away perhaps while listening to your favorite playlist. This idea is awesome because it is very kinesthetic and you can really get your whole body involved.

○ Create the board on Pinterest or another site that will enable you to do a screenshot and use it as your desktop background or your phone background. This is a great one to try if you are on your computer a lot or use your phone all the time.

Remember, the idea is to get this dream of living a *rich life full of wealth* in front of your lovely eyes as often as possible. The vision board will then attract those things to you because you will now be looking for them.

Why will you be able to see a pathway to these visions and/or goals when there did not seem to be one before? This is where it gets interesting.

There is an area of your brain called the Reticular Activating System, or RAS. It's a network of neurons that project anteriorly (toward the front) to the hypothalamus to mediate behavior, as well as both posteriorly (toward the back) to the thalamus and directly to the cortex for activation of becoming awake, desynchronized cortical EEG patterns.

Whoops, I geeked out a bit there. Let me take a moment and restate this. There are a couple of important points about the Reticular Activation System to understand.

First, this system is in the pons, which is a part of the brain stem. You can think of the brain stem as the part of your brain that keeps you alive – heart rate, breathing, and the sleep/wake cycle are all part of this system. At times, however, this part of the brain can be overreactive, for example, during an anxiety attack that comes from out of nowhere, or a racing heart when you sense that something or someone may be coming after you, even if you can't see them.

Second, the RAS filters incoming stimuli and "decides" what you should pay attention to and what is irrelevant. Here is an example:

A while back, I decided I wanted a Subaru for my next vehicle. I had seen commercials and it seemed like a good fit for our family's activities. I had not seen one on the road in my area, but I was pretty sure we could find a dealership that sold them. Indeed, before I knew it I was driving off the lot with my brand-new Subaru. And that's when things got interesting…

Once I purchased the Subaru, I saw not one or two, but five different Subarus, all the same color and model as mine!

Did they magically appear out of nowhere? No, my friends, this was my RAS in action. Because a Subaru was now something I was consciously looking for, my RAS adjusted and searched these vehicles out. Now, I see Subaru vehicles everywhere in my reality, not just in the wooded areas featured in the commercials.

The Reticular Activating System in your brain is why vision boards work. To harness the power of the RAS, we need to work on three things.

1. Make sure that creating the vision board is a fun activity! This will get your brain's attention and get the sensations in your body on board. If you have fun while you are creating the board, each time you look at it, you will remember that fun and so will your body, creating a positive physical sensation that is associated with look-ing at the vision board.

2. The board needs to be placed somewhere that you will see every day, especially when you first wake up. This will set the tone for the day, and set your RAS on the hunt for what it sees on that board. Look at your vision board as soon as you open your eyes and smile. Believe it or not, this helps the RAS to associate the vision board and its contents with positive and happy feelings, for example, excitement, comfort and safety, and so on. It all depends on the bodily sensations that are most important to you.

3. This is the hardest part, (especially for us control freaks): we need to trust and have faith that our RAS will bring our visions to us. How they come will probably surprise us, and we need to be okay with that. Faith is an important piece to this exercise. It can move moun-tains and show us unique ways to get there, if we trust the process.

Step 3:

Remember, your subconscious mind works in pictures, right? So, once you have nailed down the specific vision for a category, start looking for pictures and/or words that match that feeling. When you look at the picture, you want to feel the feeling of having it.

Please note, this will always be a work in progress. In fact, the benefit lies *in* the process. Set aside notions of making it perfect and focus instead on making it fun for yourself! Put on your favorite music and look through pictures until you find one that speaks to you. Think of it as a treasure hunt, or perhaps a quest to find your rich life full of wealth and abundance of all kinds!

Here are some suggestions of places to find pictures:

- Magazines, flyers or newspapers.
- Old books that are no longer needed.
- On the internet, for example, Bing images; Photobucket; Getty Images; and iStock. Even image clip art on Microsoft programs sometimes has the perfect picture. You can search online for free images with the phrase "Open stock images."

Remember, this process works best if you think of it as play, because play is expansive. Creating something new requires space and openness. It is best and most effective when it comes from a pure place of joy and when the process is enjoyed deeply.

Take as much time as you need. This can be an ongoing project and can look any way you want.

Another fun idea is to do this with friends. In a group, you can enjoy each other's ideas of what a rich life, full of abundance and wealth is. Just remember, community is important, so if you decide to do this in a group make sure to choose people you trust to support you in expanding your idea of becoming rich. They should lift you up and deeply believe anyone can have whatever they want because it is there for the asking.

You may be thinking, "But Suzie, I did not see you mention money once! What happened to creating a better relationship with money?" Ah, there is the key. To feel the experience of a *rich life full of abundance and wealth,* we must imagine and begin to live in that world. Obviously, we need the tool of money to support those experiences, but the experiences themselves are what fuels us and gets us excited. This vibration of excitement and joy is expansive and very attractive to the vibration of wealth.

Once we are clear on how we might experience a rich life, we will have a better idea of how much money we will need. The money itself is only a tool to assist us in creating that life.

Again, when you feel you have enough on your vision board, put it somewhere to see every day. The more you see it, the better. Remember the RAS? Looking at your vision board expands your subconscious mind to what is possible. If it makes you smile and fills your heart with joy, then and only then can we ask what amount of money is needed. So, the more you see the new possibilities as realities, the clearer your rich life will become!

We know this is possible, because it would not appear in our heart as desire or in our mind as a want or need if it was not meant for us. We only see what we desire, or what we believe. We have done the work to look at our limiting beliefs and are changing those and expanding our comfort level with money and what we deserve. We are constantly doing the work to allow more wealth in our lives. The vision board is simply another tool to remind us why we are creating this new way of being in the world -— or maybe we're just making a few tweaks because we are almost where we want to be. It keeps our focus on revamping our thoughts and reworking our neural pathways to a more abundant and prosperous life.

Our vision board is the visual anchor that reminds us we *deserve* this life. It helps us remain steadfast towards our goals. This is especially helpful when our limiting thoughts are triggered and make us uncomfortable.

Dr. Mario Martinez, author of *The Mindbody Code*, calls this feeling dissonance. We can feel it physically as a constriction in different parts of our body. Be aware of this and allow yourself to be okay with the discomfort. As you move into the new thought or idea becoming more familiar and exciting, the uncomfortable feeling will fade.

Remember, these are merely growing pains. If you can, stretch into the uncomfortable thought. See if you can view it as exciting because it signals a new phase of your life. You are growing and expanding into a more empowered and self-assured being – the person you are truly meant to be.

Creating your vision board can be a fun and exciting first step toward living a rich, abundant, and wealthy life. A life of freedom.

This may be a good time to look at the word freedom, what kind of freedom is important to you? Do you remember the top three kinds of freedom?

Let's review them.

1. Good to Great Health: A straightforward way to create wealth is to take care of your body, mind, and spirit. If you have a healthy body and mind, you are free to pursue many goals, unencumbered by doctor's appointments and prescriptions.

As I get older, this freedom speaks more loudly than ever. It has become a top goal to exercise and work on the quality of food I eat so I can continue to do the activities I love.

2. Time Abundance: This speaks to the ability to have more time to do the activities you choose throughout your day, week, year. For many, this is

the dream and a powerful motivator. If it is your goal, start allowing yourself to think outside of the box about ways to gain this freedom.

3. Social wealth: Social wealth speaks to being well connected and having a talent for connecting others. Are you a person who enjoys introducing people to each other and watching what they create together? Do you find joy in being with people and being able to see how the pieces of a powerful alliance could fit together? You may be a person who enjoys Social wealth. In many ways, this can translate into a wealthy, abundant life.

These three types of freedom are three different ways to experience wealth. Which one or do all three appeal to you? How can you speak to this type of wealth on your vision board?

Remember, this is an ongoing project. Progress is what we are after, not perfection. Above all, with this project, remember to have fun!

Chapter 8

BUILD A HEALTHY WEALTHY

Creating a Financial Team

very great journey is made better by creating a great team. Once all the work is completed, and you have started turning things around, you will find yourself with more choices. It's a natural progression from defining your meaning of rich to creating your new rich, abundant, and wealthy life.

However, to keep the momentum growing, it is important to establish a team to support this effort. If you ask any successful money manager how they make significant financial decisions, they will tell you that they never make them alone. Each person who understands that money is a tool, also knows that sometimes, emotions can get caught in the mix. This is when it is important to have trusted team members who can look at the decision objectively.

Here are some suggestions for your financial team:

Your team could be people in your family, yourself, or your spouse. It could also be people you know and trust to help you with the flow of money. Start looking at the people you know who handle money well and see if they would be willing to advise you. Perhaps they could give you suggestions or help you set up a good solid financial system. Do your research and try out a few systems and see what works. Do you have someone in your life that is a natural teacher and knows about this topic? This would be a good time to see if they are willing to help you toward financial independence.

Let's look at the following options:

1. **Financial Manager:** This person is responsible for planning and budgeting, management, and control of daily, monthly, and weekly expenses. A financial manager is also responsible for the performance measurement of investments. This job may need to be split up between two people. It all depends on how comfortable the person or persons are with this task.

   Who is the person who pays the bills and is successful in getting them paid on time consistently? You or someone else? One option is to use an automated system if you have a bank that allows you to set your bills for automatic payment. Remember you still need to monitor this process. Set a time, perhaps once a quarter or at least once a year, to review your long-term goals, and be sure to monitor them throughout the year.

   My financial manager is: _____

2. **Project Accountant:** This person is working specifically on targeted financial goals. Maybe this is the person that sets up a savings account for a given goal (perhaps a dream vacation?) and makes sure that some money gets put in that account each month. The project accountant is detail-oriented and able to see where you can save to be able to contribute to these targeted goals. Do you have someone in your family who is a saver and really excited about these goals? That person would be the best choice.

   My project accountant is: _____

3. Financial Director: This person finds the right team and systems to get the job done, and allows that team to work freely. If you or someone you trust can help with automating and tracking all your financial goals (by finding apps or other ways to make money flow easily), that person is your financial director.

Is there someone in your family who excels at research and loves setting up systems? Is this person a "big picture" person? Anyone who can help you automate your systems to create a flow to obtain greater wealth is your financial director.

My financial director is: _____

Financial Advisor: This person is probably outside of your family and needs to be the right fit for you and your financial goals. They will be your go-to person if you find the decision being made is "coming from an emotionally charged space."

How do you find this advisor? Ask friends and family to recommend people they trust. Be sure, though, to ask friends who are in the same stage of life as you because their advisors will understand your goals at this time.

Consider finding a fee-only advisor so there is no conflict of interest. You will then be at ease, knowing they are not trying to sell you a product, but will simply give you their advice.

Your advisor will become a crucial part of your community. She will be able to give you a big-picture view of how any financial decision will affect you and your family – both in terms of risks and the rewards. Because they are a key part of your financial group, you must interview them to make sure they are a good fit for your needs.

Here are some interview questions you can ask potential advisors:

1. How do you charge for your services?

   Remember this should feel safe to you. Try to find an advisor that charges a flat fee with no incentive to try to get you enrolled in a program or fee structure.

2. Are there any special fees?

   Knowing what the cost is upfront will give you peace of mind. A fee-only advisor should be able to tell you the charge for an initial consultation.

3. What licenses, credentials or other certifications do you have?

   Here are some financial advisors for you to consider:

   CPA- Certified Public Accountant: This person helps with taxes and financial analysis. CPAs take a rigorous test for their certification and stay on top of all the changes that can happen in the financial world. They will be able to advise you on how to best invest your money.

   CFP- Certified Financial Planner: CFPs have passed a difficult exam. If you have this person on your team, you can rest assured he knows how to advise you as your money and investments start to grow.

   ChFC- Chartered Financial Consultant: These people specialize in niche areas such as small business or divorce settlements. Their knowledge is narrowly focused.

   CFA- Certified Financial Analyst: A CFA is the best choice if you are looking for someone to help you with investments.

   The main goal of a certified financial analyst is to make decisions about companies, stocks and industries for the purpose of making money for a corporation or individual. CFAs track the performance of stocks and collect the data in a spreadsheet that can be interpreted by a client.

CIC- Charter Investment Counselor: This person has at least five years' experience working in investments with large portfolios, using expert investment strategies.

What is a large portfolio? A portfolio is a collection of financial investments like stocks, bonds, commodities, cash and cash equivalents (i.e., bitcoin), including closed-end funds and exchange-traded funds (ETFs). A portfolio can also include alternative investments such as real estate or anything that can grow in value or provide an income.

FRM- Financial Risk Manager: FRMs often work in banks and can assist individuals who want investment advice.

This could be a good place to start if you don't have an investment opportunity in your place of employment or are an entrepreneur and putting together your own IRA or other investment account.

CLU-Charter Life Underwriters: CLUs are experts in life insurance, estate planning and risk management. Some may have additional certifications.

4. **What services do you provide?**

Be clear about what you need. Using the list above, what seems like the best fit for you? Are you just looking for advice or do you want someone to help you manage your money? Until you get comfortable, you may want someone to advise you on money matters. As you progress, perhaps this person can help you with investments too.

5. **What types of clients do you specialize in?**

Be honest about your needs. Advisors must understand where you are currently and your future goals. If they are not the right fit for you, they may be able to suggest another advisor who would be a better match.

6. **Could I see a sample of a financial plan?**

Reviewing a sample plan is an excellent way to see if this advisor is a good fit. Are they able to explain the financial plan in a way that makes sense to you? If not, you may want to find someone else. If this is a new skill for you, it is important to have someone who is able to explain concepts in a way you can understand. Take some time to do a bit of research, maybe take a basic finance online course. Many banks offer free classes to give you the basics of the terminology. The more you know, the less intimidated you will be.

7. **What is your investment approach?**

Where are you comfortable? Are you good with being aggressive and taking risks with your money, or are you more conservative? How long do you have to reach your financial goals? If it is a long time, are you willing to take some risks? Know yourself, and what you are comfortable doing. If you know what kind of investor you are, it will be easy to tell if you and the person you interview are a match.

8. **How much contact do you have with your clients?**

Again, know yourself. Are you someone who needs a lot of attention or are you good with meeting once a year or with email updates periodically?

9. **Will I be working only with you or with a team?**

If so, can I meet the people on the team? Again, know yourself and what will make you feel secure when dealing with money decisions.

10. **What makes your client experience unique?**

It is always interesting to hear the answer to this question. Keep in mind what is important to you and see if the answer matches your concerns.

11. **Did he ask me questions and seem to be interested in me?**

You want an advisor who is invested in getting to know you and your comfort level. Keep looking if you are not feeling positive about the person you are interviewing. The right advisor is important in moving forward with your *rich life!*

Note: these came from financial expert Laura Shin's blog. I provided the link in the Resources section at the end of the book.

Take a breath and take your time, but not too much time. The sooner you get started with investing the closer you will be to reaching financial freedom. I know this is intimidating – I was sweating and getting an upset stomach as I wrote it. Here is where doing all that self-reflective work really kicks in. Understand and acknowledge that it's a little bit scary, and do it anyway!

ONE FINAL NOTE

f you have done the work presented to you in this workbook, congratulations! You are well on your way to creating a rich, abundant, and wealthy life. You now have a greater awareness of how emotions are impacting your financial decisions and know the steps to overcome unconscious blocks around money. You also have the map to create a new, healthy relationship with money and call in the lifestyle you desire. Follow the map, adjust as needed. Be brave! Doing the hard, scary stuff is how we grow into the people we are meant to be. I believe in you. You can do this!

That said, remember that this is "onion" work. You will most likely need to come back to the exercises again and again, whenever emotions have overtaken how your money is used or misused. Each time, another layer brings you closer to freeing yourself from the illusion that there is not enough money, or that it can make you happy.

Money is indeed a tool. If it is used well, many of us will find ourselves living a life in which we feel the richness of the tapestry we have created. Regardless of what others may think, in the end, *our* thoughts and beliefs are the most important.

As I write this, the minimalist and tiny home lifestyles are trending, both as means of reducing mental and physical clutter and becoming responsible stewards of our planet. People are waking up to the fact that we don't necessarily have to have stacks of cash to reach our goals. What we do need is a handle on our relationship to, and how to work with, the money we do receive.

My great hope is that you live the most abundant and *rich life* of your choosing, and that this book helps you get started on that journey.

Stay Curious!

ABOUT THE AUTHOR

Suzie McLaughlin has always had a passion for teaching. In 1985, she graduated from the University of Northern Iowa with a BA in Education and embarked on what would be a seventeen-year career in Montessori education. Later in life she became interested in another helping field, massage therapy, and eventually became an instructor at the Southwest Institute of Healing Arts in Tempe, Arizona, where she has been for the past fifteen years. It was her work helping students connect with their unique gifts and creating successful businesses in which they can grow and thrive that served as the inspiration for this book.

Suzie knew that emotions can really color how a person interacts with their world. She also realized that one of the biggest hurdles she and her students faced was around getting paid for their healing work. *Redefining Rich* was born of the need to reach more healers and help them become confident in their true worth and their ability to work with money in an empowered way.

For Suzie, balance is a big part of having a solid healing practice, and she achieves this by spending time in nature, hiking, and fishing with her family. Above all, she strives to make life an adventure in which she is always and, in all ways, truly supported – and she helps others to do the same.

Suzie is a contributing author to *The Wild Woman's Book of Shadows* compiled by Melissa Kim Corter. If you would like to purchase the book or sign up for one of Suzie's virtual or in-person classes, visit www.suziemclaughlin.com

RESOURCES

Books and Articles

Martinez, Mario E. (2014). *The Mindbody Code: How to Change the Beliefs that Limit Your Health, Longevity, and Success.* Sounds True.

Maslow, A. H. (1943). A theory of human motivation. *Psychological Review, 50*(4), 370–396.

Anodea, Judith. (1990) *Wheels of Life: A User's Guide to the Chakra System.* Llewellyn Publications.

Recommended YouTubers

Cash College https://www.youtube.com/watch?v=6zGlN4hA77g

This young man has a finance degree and is pursuing the ability to live independently (retire) by the time he is thirty-five years old. He has a lot of information that he shares in an easy-to-understand way.

Budget Girl https://www.youtube.com/watch?v=KIPq_lgXNM4

This young lady has a simple way of looking at finance and provides us with good tips on building wealth.

One Big Happy Life https://www.youtube.com/watch?v=GN3AFzXZ7kA

This couple walks us through the process of getting student loans forgiven and planning for the future. It's a solid channel with lots of great ideas.

Blogs

Shin, Laura. How to Start Earning More Money. https://www.experian.com/blogs/news/about/laura-shin/

Mr. Money Mustache. https://www.mrmoneymustache.com/

This is a great financial blog that has been around for some time and has made the Forbes top ten list again this year. It is a fun and informative site.

Made in the USA
Middletown, DE
16 April 2022

64338806R00091